HEALTH CARE CRISIS IN AMERICA

A Reference Handbook

HEALTH CARE CRISIS IN AMERICA

A Reference Handbook

Linda Brubaker Ropes

CONTEMPORARY WORLD ISSUES

ABC-CLIO

Santa Barbara, California
Denver, Colorado
Oxford, England

Library of Congress Cataloging-in-Publication Data

Ropes, Linda Brubaker, 1942–
  Health care crisis in America : a reference handbook / Linda Brubaker Ropes.
     p. cm. — (Contemporary world issues)
  Includes bibliographical references and index.
     1. Medical care—United States. 2. Medical care, Cost of—United States. 3. Right to health care—United States.   I. Title.
II. Series.
     [DNLM: 1. Delivery of Health Care—trends—United States—popular works. 2. Health Services—organization & administration—United States—directories. 3. Health Services—United States—bibliography. W 84AA1 R78h]
     RA445.R758 1991   362.1'0973—dc20   91-32913
     DNLM/DLC   for Library of Congress

ISBN 0-87436-616-X (alk. paper)

98 97 96 95 94 93 92 91   10 9 8 7 6 5 4 3 2 1

ABC-CLIO, Inc.
130 Cremona Drive, P.O. Box 1911
Santa Barbara, California 93116-1911

This book is printed on acid-free paper ∞ .
Manufactured in the United States of America

To Michael and Kathleen

Contents

Preface

THE LITERATURE ON THE HEALTH CARE CRISIS is vast, and because the field is changing so rapidly, such literature is often quickly rendered obsolete. The complexity of the crisis can be overwhelming as well. Roles are changing not only for health care professionals such as physicians, nurses, and administrators, but also for institutions. Hospitals, health maintenance organizations (HMOs), ambulatory-care centers, and home health agencies all play a part in the crisis, as do insurance carriers, pharmaceutical companies, manufacturers of medical equipment, and research centers. Add government regulations, the malpractice controversy, and a host of ethical questions, and the topic threatens to become unmanageable, especially when the experts themselves disagree on its causes—and possible solutions.

Why take on such a complex, changing, and controversial topic? Because it matters so much. On a personal level, most Americans value their health highly. As conventional wisdom has it, when you have your health, you have everything. We extend our desire for good health to our families and friends as well. On the community level, most Americans also believe that all citizens have a right to health care. Through the 1960s, that generosity of spirit served a large proportion of our population reasonably well. Congress enacted the Medicare and Medicaid programs, contriving to ensure health care for the indigent and the elderly.

Despite good intentions, however, many factors have conspired to drive health care costs increasingly higher, including expensive new technologies and the large number of elderly people. George Bernard Shaw once warned, "There are two tragedies in life. One is not to get your heart's desire. The other is to get it." In this country, our desire has been to make the best medical technology available to the greatest number of people. To a large degree, we got what we wanted, but at an enormous cost; and the cost keeps rising—as do calls to contain it. Unfortunately, most cost-containment measures also curtail access to health care. Increasing numbers of Americans have limited access to health care, inadequate care, or no care at all.

This book is an introduction to the health care crisis, which concerns us all, whether it hits us in the checkbook, the conscience, or both. It has been compiled specifically for the layperson or, more precisely, for the high school student, the undergraduate, and the general reader.

Chapter 1 is an overview of the health care crisis and the roles of the various participants in the health care system. Chapter 2 gives a brief chronology of events that have affected the health care crisis since 1960, while Chapter 3 consists of brief biographies of some of the prominent figures in the health care field. Made up of physicians, policymakers, academicians, ethicists, and lawmakers, this list includes only a few of the thousands of people who have made significant contributions to the health care field. Chapter 4 provides facts and data that reveal the extent of the crisis. Chapter 5 provides a brief list of the numerous organizations involved in health care, many of which provide publications that are excellent up-to-date resources in this ever-changing arena. A list of reference materials, books, and other print resources is presented in Chapter 6. An effort was made to provide recent literature on a broad range of topics, but again, the list is far from all-inclusive. Chapter 7 lists nonprint resources such as videos and on-line data bases. The book concludes with a glossary and an index.

Although the scope of the health care crisis is daunting, I hope readers will find that this source book provides a sense of where to begin investigating this complex problem. Throwing up our hands in a gesture of defeat is as counterproductive here as it is with any other seemingly insurmountable problem. The health care crisis must be solved. I do not want to imagine a society where only the wealthy have access to adequate health care, which seems to be where current trends are taking us. If that dismal event occurs, the rising cost of health care will have truly bankrupted our nation—not only fiscally, but morally as well.

Acknowledgments

THIS BOOK IS THE RESULT of nearly a year of research and would have been impossible to compile without the generous assistance of many people. I would like to thank the librarians of Jefferson County Library and Denver Public Library for their unfailingly cheerful and able assistance. In particular, I wish to thank those who shared their time and expertise by reviewing sections of this book for accuracy and completeness. Reviewers included Thomas P. Weil, Ph.D.; William L. Kissick, M.D.; John Sbarbaro, M.D.; and Richard D. Lamm. Thanks also to Len Wheeler, M.D., who provided insight into what it is like to be a physician in today's health care system. I am deeply grateful to my editor, Heather Cameron, for her vigilance to detail and for her many helpful suggestions and encouragement. And last, but by no means least, thanks to my husband for his patience, support, and understanding.

1

Overview of the Health Care Crisis

ALTHOUGH THE UNITED STATES CONTINUES to lead the world in the development of new medical technology, its health care system is in a state of crisis. Contradictions abound. Organ transplants and other dramatic procedures arouse the emotional applause of the populace; yet to be a minority, less educated, or poor is to be subject to more suffering, disability, and premature death than other Americans.

Cost and Access

Rising costs and unequal access to care are two of the most frequently cited symptoms of the health care crisis. In 1990, Americans spent an estimated $660 billion on health care, which is almost 12 percent of our gross national product (GNP). This compares with 9.1 percent in 1980 and under 6 percent prior to the introduction of Medicare and Medicaid in the mid-1960s. In 1987, per capita health care expenditures in the United States, at over $2,050, were double the average for the next six largest industrial countries—Canada, France, Germany, Italy, Japan, and the United Kingdom. (Figures from 1987 are the most recent figures available.) And yet, with such high expenditures, the United States ranks only eighth in the world in life expectancy, eleventh in maternal mortality, eighteenth in child mortality, and twenty-second in infant mortality. Two out of every five American children, and four out of every five minority children, have not been properly immunized against common diseases.

An estimated 37 million Americans, approximately 15 percent of the population, have no health insurance, while another 30 percent of the population have only minimal coverage. Access to health care is denied not only to the poor, the working poor, and their dependents, but to rural dwellers as well. Some 16 million rural citizens live in counties with few or no health care services. Lacking insurance or the ability to pay high deductibles, many Americans skip regular checkups and avoid seeking medical care when problems first arise. Lack of preventive care, especially prenatal and well baby care, can cost much more in direct health care costs later on if problems go untreated.

Our health care system is a hodgepodge of 1,500 third-party payers and programs; this leads to overlaps or immense gaps in care, duplicative paperwork, and cost-shifting practices among payers. Administrative costs gobble up between 22 and 25 cents of every health care dollar, while other Western industrial countries pay about 10 cents on the dollar. In addition to these problems, there are numerous other interrelated factors that complicate the health care crisis, including increased malpractice litigation, a tax system that gives employees tax-free health benefits, the continuing nursing shortage, the long-term-care and acute-care needs of our aging population, ethical dilemmas, the yet-to-be-determined cost of the AIDS epidemic, and our unrealistic expectations about what health care can achieve.

Although change has always characterized health care in the United States, the rate of change has accelerated in the last 25 years. In the first seven decades of this century, three factors remained fairly constant: the dominance of the medical profession; local sponsorship of community hospitals; and cross-subsidization, which allowed physicians and hospitals to care for many of the poor by overcharging the wealthy. Medicare and Medicaid legislation was passed in 1965 because the aged could no longer afford health care, and because the Robin Hood system of supporting the poor by increasing charges to the wealthy was breaking down. Many experts see the enactment of this legislation as a major turning point that eroded the stability of the former system. In the years since its passage, for-profit and not-for-profit hospital systems have come to threaten the role of many autonomous community hospitals. In addition, the broad risk pool that helped the sick to obtain health insurance at a reasonable cost is segmenting more and more as large employers move to self-insurance. General health insurance for people who do not belong to a specific group is becoming increasingly expensive.

Role of Physicians

The expanded role of physicians is one of the major changes in the health care system. As William Kissick, M.D., of the University of Pennsylvania puts it, "From deity to Marcus Welby to mere mortal in less than a generation is a steep fall from grace." (From an article in *Hospital and Health Services Administration* 33 [Fall 1988]: 3.) Social, political, and legal forces are confronting physicians with ethical and economic problems unheard of even a decade ago. Their style of practice is evolving from the solo fee-for-service model to a group setting, sometimes on a salaried basis. Conflicts of interest arise as physicians share financial risks with insurers, or even become investors in the very health care services or facilities where they practice. Their autonomy is threatened, and their incomes are not likely to be as high as they once were. In an increasingly competitive climate, with their numbers in oversupply, physicians must justify major clinical decisions to third-party payers and managers. They find themselves obligated to balance clinical considerations not only against a patient's financial welfare, but also against society's judgment that health care expenditures are too high.

Trained to put a patient's medical welfare above all else, physicians are increasingly confronted with pressures to cut costs. Cost-containment measures and pressures to increase revenues can and do put patients at risk. Medicare's system of prospective payment, for example, which reimburses hospitals with a fixed payment per admission based on a diagnosis-related group (DRG), can lead hospitals to encourage physicians to readmit patients for second procedures that could have been performed during prior admissions. In another strategy to increase revenue, called "DRG creep," physicians may be encouraged to place patients into more lucrative categories by making it look as if they are sicker than they actually are; or physicians may be urged to discharge patients before they are ready, only to readmit them a short time later under new diagnoses, so the hospital will receive more reimbursement. An additional cost-saving ploy is to send severely ill and potentially unprofitable patients to other hospitals, which are often municipally owned.

Malpractice Litigation

The constant threat of malpractice litigation plagues modern physicians. The trend toward more litigation has been increasing since the 1970s and began accelerating in the mid-1980s. In addition to an increase in the number of suits, the amounts awarded by judges and juries to successful claimants have gone up as well. This escalation of malpractice litigation has significant consequences for society as well as for physicians. Taxpayers must support the legal system that processes these lawsuits, and malpractice insurance premium costs are driven up. In addition, the doctors are forced to practice "defensive medicine," which increases health care costs. In order to protect themselves in the event of a lawsuit, physicians cover every act with extensive written documentation and order more tests than are clinically necessary. Although estimates vary, as much as $15 billion to $40 billion annually may be spent on defensive medical care.

When the malpractice crisis first hit in the mid-1970s, several major insurance companies pulled out of the medical market. Those that remained increased their premiums as much as 300 percent, and for some specialists such as obstetricians and neurosurgeons, as much as 500 percent. Today, the cost for malpractice insurance varies widely depending on specialty, geographic area, and other factors. Some neurosurgeons practicing in New York City pay over $100,000 annually for malpractice coverage. Such exorbitant costs are inevitably passed along to patients.

Defenders of the U.S. legal system point out that some positive results have come from physicians changing their practice patterns in response to the threat of malpractice suits. They may keep better records, spend more time with patients, and refer out difficult cases. On the other hand, the threat of malpractice has also negatively impacted the patient-physician relationship. Operating in a climate of patient distrust is a quantum leap from the days when most Americans would never have dreamed of questioning their physicians, let alone suing them. Many malpractice experts believe that the current tendency to sue is far more related to patients' anger over the impersonality of the system than to a desire for financial reward.

Many experts in the health care field are calling for tort reform, and some states have responded by enacting legislation that sets a cap on awards and reduces awards by the amount of other sources of insurance. No malpractice legislation has been passed nationally. Meanwhile, Americans continue to absorb the costs of higher malpractice insurance premiums in their medical bills, and they sometimes lose the services of highly trained specialists who leave the field or a specific location in the face of high insurance rates.

Role of Nurses

As the role of physicians is changing radically in the face of the health care crisis, so is the role of nurses. The American Nurses Association reports that nurses desire more autonomy, better pay, enhanced educational opportunities, and improved staffing patterns. Today's professional nurses are less willing to waste their professional skills on menial tasks. As much as 50 percent of a registered nurse's time is currently spent on clerical, house-keeping, and other routine activities that could be performed by others. The dedicated nurse who unflinchingly works long hours for low pay may soon be as extinct as the doctor who makes house calls.

Since the early 1980s, an increased demand has led to a nursing shortage, which has had a negative impact on the quality of care in many hospitals, long-term-care institutions, and other facilities. On the average, the nation's more than two million registered nurses earn $28,383 a year. Their average starting salary of $24,604 compares favorably with that of many other professions, but the pay rates tend to reach maximum levels five to ten years after nurses enter the field. The average maximum pay for experienced nurses is far below that for many other professionals. According to the U.S. Department of Labor, accountants, for example, can expect a 209 percent salary progression during the course of their careers, while registered nurses can expect only a 69 percent increase. In addition to desiring better pay, many members of the nursing profession resent the relatively low status they hold in light of their education and responsibility level. The shortage of nurses may continue if some of their concerns are not addressed by the health care community.

Health Insurance

In addition to changing the roles of health care professionals, the health care crisis is affecting businesses, which now contribute a staggeringly high percentage of their revenues to insure the health of their employees. Although over half of the country's big businesses have adopted or are considering adopting self-insurance policies, small businesses are increasingly forced to choose between paying high insurance premiums or offering their employees no coverage at all. Those employees who are insured are paying increasingly higher prices for their coverage, and most conventional policies do not cover preventive services or long-term chronic care for any extended period. This lack of coverage for long-term care is an increasing problem in our aging society. Growing numbers of the elderly are forced to deliberately pauperize themselves to become eligible for Medicaid benefits.

Most experts agree that the third-party payment system for insurance encourages overuse of the health care system. The federally financed Health Insurance Experiment conducted by the Rand Corporation from 1974 to 1982 found that members of families with lower cost-sharing percentages in their insurance plans visited physicians more frequently and entered the hospital more often than members of families who had higher copayments or deductibles. On the basis of this and other studies, one expert concluded that a typical, relatively comprehensive insurance policy approximately doubles the demand for services. In addition, perverse tax incentives compound the problem. Since the money an employer spends on purchasing health insurance for workers is excluded from taxable income, workers tend to view health insurance plans as tax-free compensation, rather than as real income.

Cost-Containment Efforts

In response to these incentives to demand more expensive services, a variety of efforts to control costs have been made by the government, private insurers, and employers. The most common methods are to provide fewer benefits at the same premium price and to increase the required payments for coinsurance and deductibles. Capitation plans are increasingly being tried in an effort to control health care costs as well. These plans reverse the traditional insurance scheme of paying on a fee-for-service basis after the care has been delivered. With capitation, health care providers are paid in advance on a per capita basis for patients committed to using their services. Health maintenance organizations (HMOs) are the predominant form of this arrangement, although not all of them are capitated, such as independent-practice associations, which now account for four out of every ten HMO enrollees. Capitated coverage has the advantage of offering preventive care; however, critics of HMOs point out that such providers must take steps to prevent the "more-is-better" incentive of such programs by lengthening the waiting time for nonemergency appointments or placing other nonmonetary barriers before patients.

Although, theoretically, patients required to pay more for their care will seek less of it, increased patient cost sharing has had only a moderate effect on medical costs, especially hospital costs. There are limits to how much cost sharing can achieve. It may decrease patients' use of health care, but it can also decrease their access to needed care. Waiting to seek medical attention may prevent the early identification and treatment of diseases, which may then be more expensive to treat in the long run.

Role of Hospitals

The changes that have occurred in hospitals since the advent of Medicare and Medicaid are closely tied to the changes experienced by physicians, nurses, and insurance providers. The sudden increase in third-party payments to hospitals by government programs lessened the hospitals' long-standing preoccupation with financial concerns. The new strong cash flows enabled hospitals to break away from the philanthropic sources they depended on in the past and borrow the money they needed for expansion, improvements, and modernization. In addition, the third-party payment system underwent rapid growth, with the share of personal health costs paid by governments and private insurance almost doubling between 1950 and 1970. For-profit hospital chains expanded, giving rise to unfounded fears that they would take over the market; however, they have never occupied more than 15 percent of the marketplace.

By the early 1970s, what Eli Ginzberg, Ph.D., of Columbia University calls "the monetarization of health care" was well under way. With federal dollars flowing into hospitals, the basis of health care shifted from the human service sector to a money-driven industrial model. However, alarmed at the rapidly growing costs of health care programs, the federal government began to take a more aggressive role in cost containment. In the 1970s, it established professional standards review organizations (PSROs) and certificate-of-need legislation in an attempt to place a ceiling on annual capital outlays for hospitals. When President Reagan took office in 1981, the new administration announced that it would rely on the competitive market strategy, rather than on federal regulation, to shape the nation's health care system. This encouraged the rapid growth of entrepreneurial activities. HMOs, preferred provider organizations (PPOs), and other forms of managed care proliferated; large corporations moved increasingly to self-insurance; and ambulatory-care facilities sprouted up all over the United States.

However, regulation was soon reinstituted in an effort to contain costs. Medicare introduced the prospective-payment system using DRGs in 1983. This system for reimbursing hospitals eliminated cost-based retrospective reimbursement in favor of prospective payment based on classification of care. The hospital receives the same payment per DRG, with some exceptions, regardless of how long the patient stays or the actual cost of the care provided. If the DRG payment exceeds the cost of care, the hospital can keep the excess; however, if the cost of care exceeds the DRG level, the hospital has to absorb the loss.

Faced with this belt-tightening measure and increasing competition, many hospitals became more inclined to "dump" patients with limited or no insurance on public hospitals. Legislation to curb this trend was passed, as was a law forbidding hospitals to turn poor patients away at the emergency room before they were "stabilized." This may be humane, but it has created a financial burden for hospitals. For example, in 1989, the typical bill for a trauma patient was $13,000. On average, hospitals took a loss of $5,000 on each patient. Although trauma is the leading cause of death for people under age 44, killing more than 140,000 people in the United States each year, many hospitals are shifting resources away from emergency care out of economic necessity.

Large urban hospitals with fully equipped emergency rooms are not the only ones facing potential closure; rural and small inner-city hospitals are struggling to survive as well. A decline in the number of hospitals will create a crisis for the already beleaguered poor, for whom the emergency room has become the primary source of care.

Other financial forces are likely to force hospital closures in the future. Due to aggressive cost-containment efforts, hospital admissions and lengths of stay have been falling since the mid-1980s. As a result, for-profit hospitals that are owned, leased outright, or sponsored by large corporations had 110,330 beds in 1989, down from 115,721 in 1987. Predictions that they would take over the hospital market appear to be unfounded. Although Medicare's DRG system played a significant role in the decline in hospital admissions and lengths of stay, other factors were also involved. Peer review organizations that assess the necessity of hospital admission, the growth of various forms of ambulatory care, and an overall increased cost-consciousness have also contributed. Since keeping enrollees out of the hospital saves insurers money, they have begun to provide coverage for ambulatory care outside the hospital setting. Medical technology has also contributed to this trend by making it possible for some 40 percent of surgical procedures to be safely performed in ambulatory settings. Lasers, for example, minimize cutting and blood loss, while improved anesthetics allow patients to go home clear-headed shortly after waking up.

In addition to out-of-hospital surgery, ambulatory care offers other forms of less expensive care with greater accessibility. These include freestanding centers for emergency care, urgent care, and convenience care. Urgent-care centers, for example, charge less than hospital emergency rooms, so insurers create reimbursement incentives to encourage their use. This helps explain the growth of "doc in the box" centers in U.S. suburbs. These centers do not maintain the expensive standby equipment and personnel found in hospitals. If patients are seriously ill, they are transferred to hospitals. With their lower overhead costs and lower prices, urgent-care centers are an advantage to patients and insurance companies, but certainly not to already struggling hospitals. In an effort to compete, some hospitals are responding by operating their own lower-priced centers adjacent to their emergency rooms or elsewhere near patients who can afford to pay.

Hospital profits have also been affected by the increasing use of home health care. With our aging population, this trend is likely to increase dramatically. Medical technology has fostered the growth of the home health care industry with the introduction of portable intravenous equipment, which now makes it possible to administer antibiotics, chemotherapy, and nutrition in patients' homes. As the demand for home health care increases, hospitals are responding by expanding into this market as well. Lobbying attempts by organizations representing the elderly are seeking to increase Medicare funding for home health care, and some insurers are beginning to extend their coverage for such services.

Effects of Regulation

Many of the attempts to address the health care crisis have led to unexpected and often negative results. The altruistic intent behind Medicare and Medicaid, for example, was commendable, but the effects have reached far beyond providing health care for the elderly and the poor. One unforeseen legacy of those programs was the fragmenting of much of the health care system. For-profit hospitals, public hospitals, rural providers, and urban hospitals have all become separate interest groups and formed lobbies of their own. Medicare's conflicting payment incentives for hospitals and physicians promoted a divergence in their interests, and the medical lobby itself began to disintegrate. Specialty societies have gained strength, while the once powerful American Medical Association (AMA) no longer represents the majority of U.S. physicians. In addition to giving rise to multiple health care lobbies, Medicare and Medicaid have also bred numerous new health care settings and providers by encouraging health care to move out of the expensive hospital setting. Despite the goal to lower costs through the use of such decentralized facilities, total spending has continued to rise almost unabated.

Other forms of federal regulation and legislation have profoundly affected the health care system. A perceived shortage of physicians in the 1950s led to legislation that encouraged enrollment in the nation's medical schools. Now in the 1990s the nation is experiencing a glut of physicians at a time when the medical marketplace is already fiercely competitive. Many medical schools, and especially their teaching hospitals, are now in financial trouble. During the flush era of the 1950s and 1960s, Congress poured money into research and development programs at the National Institutes of Health (NIH). Comparatively, funding in the last two decades has slowed to a trickle, yet the need for research has not lessened, especially in view of the AIDS epidemic.

Pharmaceutical companies complain that legislation allowing the sale of generic drugs puts them at a disadvantage. They claim that they must charge higher prices than generic drug manufacturers to cover the cost of research and development. But critics of the pharmaceutical industry are quick to point out that it is one of the most profitable industries in the country.

Controversy rages as to which sectors of the health care system are contributing the most to the crisis. Rising costs have received the bulk of attention as the most visible measure of malaise. The majority of the attempts at cost containment have failed, however, partly because they are swimming upstream against a powerful tide of technological and demographic changes. As soon as business or government comes up with a new way to purchase a service or equipment for a better price, an upgrade occurs, and yesterday's technology is rendered obsolete. In addition, our aging population requires more and more care.

After a new regulation is instituted, it takes very little time for cost shifting to begin. No cost-containment measure to date has come up with a new source of funds; it has merely shifted the burden to someone else, such as big business, whose health insurance premium costs have risen rapidly due to cost-shifting tactics. Not only have sporadic measures at cost containment been largely unsuccessful, but they are also fragmented and lack any cohesive guiding policy, prompting many leaders in the health care field to plead for a national health care policy or a national health insurance plan.

Effects of Competition

When regulation did not staunch the flow of health care dollars, competition was touted as the answer to the crisis. The "managed-care" concept of HMOs and PPOs produced initial savings, but the costs of these systems seemed to rise at approximately the same rate as the costs of unmanaged care. In 1990, 13.9 percent of the population belonged to HMOs; this represents a significant change, but less than managed-care industry leaders were predicting in the early 1980s. The 3.9 percent rise in HMO enrollments to 35 million in 1989 was a slowing from the 8.7 percent increase in 1988, which had been the slowest rate of increase in HMO membership since the early 1980s. Fewer HMOs were under development at the end of 1989 than at any time since the mid-1970s, when passage of federal legislation spurred the growth of the industry.

Opinions about the success of managed care vary greatly. Some argue that HMOs, PPOs, and similar systems bring new services to populations presently lacking them, forcing greater efficiencies in hospitals and in the health care industry in general. Others contend that these profit-oriented ventures serve only profitable patients with profitable illnesses and leave higher-risk patients or those with nonprofitable conditions to the public sector. In addition, critics claim that health care does not readily fit into the classic supply-and-demand model of economic theory. The creation of a purely competitive marketplace for health care is based on presumptions that may not be true. Most patients have only the power to choose a physician, hospital, or health plan; they have no way of making an informed choice about the details of their health care because they have no way of knowing which choice will yield the best results. In most instances, they lack the knowledge or the time to make an informed choice, as in the case of a medical emergency.

Although the free-market concept of health care has staunch advocates, opponents cite the tendency of a profit motive to diminish people's trust in a service, and health care is an area in which trust is essential. Some fear that this emerging system, called the "medical-industrial complex" by Arnold S. Relman, M.D., editor of the *New England Journal of Medicine,* may strike a critical blow to the doctor-patient relationship. Seeing health as a commodity may lead to a shift in values, causing a diminution of compassion in the health care profession.

Bioethics

Compassion is called upon frequently these days as modern technology makes it necessary for health care professionals to assist in making ethical decisions in situations that did not exist a few years ago. As our resources become more limited, who is to decide, and on what basis, who will live and who will die? Is the life of a 90-year-old, senile post-stroke widow in a nursing home of equal value to that of a one-pound premature infant on a life-support system in the intensive-care unit of a children's hospital?

With the increase in the number of the elderly, such predicaments will only worsen. Currently, 30 million people, or 12 percent of all U.S. citizens, are over age 65. By 2030, the over-65 citizenry will number 65 million, or 21 percent of the population. Plus the over-85 generation is the fastest growing population segment in the United States. This aging population will need both acute and chronic care, and as our current system stands, many of them will have to drain their life savings to pay for it. With our ability to prolong life, many of them and their families will face agonizing moral decisions about whether and when to withdraw life-support systems. Daniel Callahan, one of the nation's leading medical ethicists and director of the Hastings Center, believes that we must grapple with the provocative argument that living longer is not necessarily better. He would have Congress restrict Medicare payments for such procedures as organ transplants, heart bypasses, and kidney dialysis for the aged, believing that there are better ways to spend money than indefinitely extending life. Like former Colorado Governor Richard Lamm, Callahan believes that long-term treatment of the elderly drains funds from the health needs of other groups and from urgent social problems. As Lamm puts it, "We cannot afford a system where on our way out the door, we take $100,000 to $200,000 of our children's limited resources to give us a couple of extra days of pain-wracked existence. Such a practice is more than bad policy, it is intergenerational larceny." ("The Brave New

World of Health Care," address delivered to the Affordable Health Care Forum 4 October 1990 in Denver, CO.)

Modern medical technology gives rise to a host of ethical questions, not only for the elderly, but for all citizens. Amazing advances in human genetic intervention, reproductive technology, and biomedical intervention are challenging traditional values at an accelerating rate. Whether to treat seriously ill newborn infants aggressively is one of the most difficult decisions facing the health care community today. These tiny patients are so utterly dependent, with no say of their own, unlike mature patients who can express their opinions about the course of their care or who may have signed a living will. The average cost per survivor for a 500- to 900-gram infant is nearly $200,000. In the last decade, the U.S. press has publicized the painful struggles over ethical decisions that used to be made in private. The courts have intervened in cases of surrogate motherhood, the right of parents to request the withdrawal of life-support systems from their irreversibly comatose children, and many other ethical dilemmas. In our pluralistic society, finding answers to satisfy everyone is a daunting task. Some issues, such as abortion, have become highly politicized in the process.

Although the concept of rationing is anathema to most Americans, rationing is presently occurring by default. We are already spending vast amounts of money on some people and virtually none on others. For example, we spend about $3 billion a year on neonatal intensive care, while we deny prenatal care to hundreds of thousands of women. We spend $50 billion a year on people in the last six months of their lives, while we close pediatric clinics because we claim we do not have the resources to keep them open. Prioritizing where limited health care dollars go has other repercussions as well. If, for example, health care reforms respond to the problems of cost and access, it is likely that research and development and the diffusion of new technologies may be slowed, possibly harming the quality of care.

British and Canadian Health Care Systems

To correct these inequities, numerous proposals have been made to support various forms of national health insurance for the

United States. Some are modeled after the British and Canadian systems, while others are more innovative in their approach. Created in 1948 as the free world's first comprehensive government health care system, the British National Health Service is now one of the world's largest employers. In 1989, it had one million employees, including over 50,000 physicians. General tax revenues finance the system, which provides health services from the cradle to the grave for all British citizens. They have access to general practitioners, although not necessarily one of their choosing, at no charge and can obtain prescription drugs at a nominal cost. No charges are made for hospital care, physician visits, or tests. Although all citizens are eligible for the health service, approximately 10 percent of Britons choose to pay for private care instead.

The Canadian system, often touted as the model the United States could most readily emulate, is more decentralized than the one in Britain. Since 1971, all of Canada's provinces have provided universal hospital and physician insurance. The amount contributed by the federal government varies from province to province. Health care funding is channeled through provincial health care programs, and citizens have a free choice of hospitals and doctors. Funding sources for the provincial portion of the system vary: In some provinces, funding comes from a mixture of income and sales taxes; in others, funding is based on social insurance principles, with residents required to pay premiums. Most of the hospital beds in Canada are in not-for-profit institutions, with the insurance program in each province reimbursing hospitals for their operating costs. All physicians' fees are fixed.

Those looking to foreign models as a quick fix for the United States' health care crisis will find that on closer scrutiny, those systems also have their problems. Ironically, one of the same factors driving up our health care costs is also associated with social insurance and national health systems: Patients who make little or no contribution to the cost of their care make unlimited demands. The only way to curb the rising demand when prices are kept artificially low is to control the prices or impose rationing. To one degree or another, both Britain and Canada have resorted to both of these tactics. Britain imposes income controls on physicians, which has kept down the health care budget, but has led to some emigration by physicians and frequent strikes by medical personnel. Britain has one of the lowest ratios of physicians to people—one physician to 1,000 people—of any Western industrialized country. If it were not for immigration by doctors from Third World countries where salaries are lower than those in Britain, its doctor-patient ratio would be even lower. Canada has resorted to increasingly stringent controls over physicians' fees to keep costs reasonable.

Low pay for medical personnel is not the only problem in the British and Canadian systems. Direct rationing is a way of life. In Canada, for example, deterioration of facilities, shortages of new equipment, and waiting lists are gradually intensifying. Long waiting lists for elective treatments in Canada trouble patients and physicians alike, since such a situation denies the ideal of national health care. Patients in Vancouver can expect to wait as long as nine months for a cataract operation, while a corneal transplant might involve a delay of as much as four years. In Britain, rationing by imposing a waiting list for nonemergency surgery has become extreme. Even urgent cases may have to wait well over a year for major eye or orthopedic surgery. Such waits can be more than inconvenient; they can be fatal.

Americans are not likely to accept the waiting lists and other shortcomings of such systems. For decades, Congress has resisted numerous attempts to pass a national health insurance plan. Many observers criticize the quality of health care provided by the Veterans Administration, which has its own separate system of hospitals and physicians. Alain Enthoven, Ph.D., of Stanford University summarizes the fears of many Americans with this statement: "You might say the people who brought us the savings and loan fiasco and the HUD fiasco and the nuclear weapons plants and the scandals and cost overruns in national defense are not going to turn around and bring us a good, cost-effective health insurance program." (Stated on "Business World," an ABC News program, 14 January 1990.) Yet as the health care crisis continues unabated, many observers believe that reform of some kind must occur. Proposed legislation for at least a universal access plan and maybe eventually a national health insurance plan is before Congress again this year. Although experts disagree over what is politically possible, economically feasible, and socially just, a rising number agree that some measures must be taken. The search is still under way for health care reform that will provide adequate access for the poor and yet control costs.

Wellness and Preventive Care

National health insurance or some other form of legislation is not the only change that could affect the health care crisis. Programs emphasizing wellness and preventive care could contribute to the health of the nation as well as cut costs. At the present time, no coordinated effort is being made to educate the public about the necessity of preventive measures and the impact that changes in life-style could have on health care costs.

The main reasons people die before their time today are clear: cigarettes, diet, alcohol, gunshots, and the nonuse of seat belts. Approximately two-thirds of all deaths before age 65 are essentially self-imposed. Diet is a prime factor in heart disease, which kills hundreds of thousands of Americans a year; cigarettes claim 360,000 lives, and alcohol and drugs kill at least 100,000 annually.

Ambivalence of Americans

Americans are schizophrenic when it comes to making demands from the health care system. We seem to want more care, the latest technology, and more personal attention, but are increasingly unwilling to pay for it. We refuse to recognize that the technology we value so highly is on a collision course with scarcity. Our conflicting values lead to the generous support of such expenditures as the national renal dialysis program, which costs an average of $25,000 per patient per year, but we are unwilling to support taxes to provide more adequate health care for the poor. Why should citizens who happen to have kidney disease receive public support when those with hundreds of other debilitating diseases receive little or no support at all?

As technology advances and more medical successes occur, people tend to transfer hope into need. One hundred years ago, no one "needed" a heart transplant, because such a possibility did not exist. U.S. society tends to believe that ultimately everything can be fixed, including our health, and that we all have a right to unlimited health care. We refuse to accept illness and death as inevitable parts of life, and this unrealistic expectation gets us into trouble as costs spiral and more people are denied access to adequate care. No matter how much progress is made, doctors' offices will always be full, and death and suffering will continue. Despite our infatuation with science and technology, not all medical problems will be conquered; new medical frontiers will always exist. Some experts believe that we need to shift our attention away from individual needs and toward what is good for the community as a whole. Changing public attitudes is no easy task, but it is no less daunting than tackling the myriad other problems contributing to the health care crisis. In a multifaceted system that is so complex and changing so rapidly, finding a solution to the crisis will be difficult at best.

However, finding a workable solution to the health care crisis is crucial for all Americans. In our personal lives, each of us is affected by our health or our lack thereof. We have come to expect access to quality care at a reasonable cost, yet for millions of Americans that expectation is no longer a reality. To deny even one citizen the opportunity to receive adequate health care is to deny the equality our nation has valued for over 200 years. What is known about the immensely complicated problem of the health care crisis cannot easily be condensed into one volume, but this source book is designed to provide a starting point to help those searching for solutions.

2

Chronology

THE FOLLOWING IS A CHRONOLOGY of significant events, legislation, judicial decisions, and scientific discoveries since 1960 that are related to the health care crisis in the United States. Dramatic improvements have characterized the development of health care in the twentieth century. In the first half of the century, the most significant discoveries led to the prevention and cure of infectious diseases. Researchers developed vaccines to prevent such deadly scourges as yellow fever and measles. The discovery of antibiotics saved thousands of lives, and technological advances such as the heart-lung machine opened the door to previously impossible surgical techniques.

By today's standards, those first advances in health care seem painstakingly slow. For example, although penicillin was discovered in 1929, it was not available for widespread use until 1941. Since the 1960s, the rate of technological advance has increased so rapidly that the announcement of new discoveries is commonplace today. However, the irony of our times is that although health care has never been better, fewer Americans have access to it. Many factors, including the expense of new technology, rising health insurance rates, and the demands of an aging population, have led to a rationing of health care based on the ability to pay. Costs continue to rise. In 1989, medical care costs in the United States rose at a rate approximately two times the rate of inflation.

Accompanying the concerns over access to health care and rising costs are numerous ethical questions arising from the new capabilities of modern technology. The greater capacity to prolong or save lives also creates questions about the quality of life, the right to die, and other ethical dilemmas. Complex ethical decisions have become so commonplace that a few hospitals now have ethical specialists on their staffs.

The following chronology is a selected list of the significant events since the 1960s that have been landmarks in or contributed to the current health care crisis.

1960   The Sabin oral vaccine for polio, successfully tested in the U.S.S.R., is administered in the United States, effectively wiping out the peril of polio. This dramatic advance contributes to rising expectations in U.S. society that eventually all major medical problems can be conquered.

1960– 1963   Mild tranquilizers, such as Librium and Valium, are introduced. These benzodiazepines are widely prescribed, becoming popularly known as "the martini of the 1960s." Americans come to expect modern medicine to not only cure disease, but enhance their emotional state as well. Increasingly, the United States becomes a nation that turns to pills to solve problems. By 1989, Americans spend approximately $29 billion a year on prescription drugs and $16 billion on nonprescription drugs.

1961   The birth-control pill is first used. Based on synthetic progesterone, "the pill," as it comes to be called, prevents pregnancy by suppressing ovulation in women. It remains the most widely used, convenient, and effective birth-control method to date.

1964   The first successful heart bypass operation is performed. The surgeon removes a vein from the patient's leg and attaches it to the heart to provide a new route for the flow of blood.

New York is the first state to adopt a certificate-of-need law, which requires state approval for hospital construction. By 1972, 23 states and the District of Columbia adopt similar legislation, stating that decisions should be based on state and areawide plans. This variance of laws from state to state is one of many examples of decentralization within the U.S. health care system. Planning is haphazard and often left in the hands of the states. Access to health care remains partly a function of where a citizen happens to live.

1965   An amendment to the Health Professions Educational Assistance Act encourages medical schools to double their graduates

1965
cont.
as a means of curtailing costs. The scarcity of physicians turns into an oversupply in some parts of the country, but the cost of medical care continues to rise.

National legislation sets up Medicaid and Medicare programs. Medicaid is a federal/state program for the indigent and the medically indigent in which each state administers its own program and determines its own eligibility requirements. The federal share is based on a formula involving per capita income in the state. Medicare is a federal health insurance program for hospitalization for the elderly financed by Social Security taxes. Medicare also includes payment for physicians' fees and other services financed through a monthly premium paid by the enrollee and federal tax revenues. The first full year of Medicare in 1966 costs $4.7 billion to cover 19 million people. In 1990, the federal government budgets $94.9 billion for Medicare to cover 33 million people. Today, the cost of this program is making deep inroads into the Social Security fund.

1967
The first human heart transplant is performed. Over 300 patients receive heart transplants within the next nine years, but most of them die within a year of the operation. At first the media sensationalize the procedure, but by the late 1970s, heart transplants are in disrepute and fewer and fewer are performed. This is one operation in which the short-term benefits for the patient are outweighed by the cost in the public's mind. However, with their higher success rates, liver transplants increase in the 1970s and 1980s. Access to this expensive operation is limited to those who can afford to pay, raising ethical questions about equity.

1968
A vaccine for spinal meningitis, an inflammation of the membrane covering the brain and spinal cord, is discovered. From the mid-1940s to the early 1960s, sulfa drugs keep meningitis under control. All at once, however, the sulfa drugs lose their effectiveness. An epidemic on Navy bases in California in 1962 and 1963 leads to a crash program to develop a vaccine. Once again, the U.S. public's expectations are raised about possible medical advances with no consideration of cost.

1969
Elisabeth Kübler-Ross publishes *On Death and Dying*. This classic study on the emotional responses of dying patients elevates the subject of death and dying to a new plateau, attempting to lift the taboo against talking about death in U.S. society. However, most Americans still cling to the belief that modern technology will someday conquer most, if not all, health problems.

1960s The National Institutes of Health (NIH) campaign against childhood leukemia leads to success with the combination of medications and radiation. The leukemia survival rate for children rises from 4 percent in the early 1960s to 65 percent by the 1980s. Post World War II to the mid-1960s is the heyday of congressional funding for NIH. Lobbying and other forms of political persuasion play a major role in what forms of research are funded and for how much.

1960s– The U.S. Public Health Service National Health Service Corps
1970s finances medical education for graduates who promise to serve two years in urban or rural areas with special needs. The Reagan administration drastically cuts back on this program, promoting the idea that putting health care on the open competitive market will reduce costs. Cutting back the Service Corps program reduces costs, but further limits the access of many indigent Americans to primary-care physicians.

1971 Congress enacts major amendments to the Health Professions Educational Assistance Act as a result of growing concern that the nation faces a serious physician shortage. This legislation introduces the principle of capitation payments to medical schools that are not conditional upon reciprocal additions to the annual pool of graduates. In two decades, the effect of this act is to create an oversupply of physicians in some geographical areas and in some specialties. Fewer doctors enter family practice and other primary-care specialties. With increased competition, more physicians work for a salary than ever before. As more physicians work for organizations, critics charge that the quality of the physician-patient relationship erodes as the doctor becomes more business oriented.

1972 The computerized axial tomography (CAT; also called CT) scan is invented. The CT scan is designed to overcome the flaw of regular x-rays, which cannot distinguish one soft tissue from another. This expensive diagnostic tool is installed in hospitals nationwide. In the increasingly competitive medical marketplace, several hospitals in one community often own CT scanners. Costs rise for hospitals and for the insurers that pay for the increased use of this new technology.

Responding to the need to clarify ethical questions, the American Hospital Association issues a declaration about patients' rights. It includes the right of informed consent to treatment and to the patient's right to privacy. Accreditation by the Joint Commission on Accreditation of Hospitals hinges on following

1972
cont.
these guidelines, so the commission helps to enforce them; however, no one checks to see how well a hospital's bill of rights is enforced.

An amendment to Social Security legislation provides life-saving treatment for all U.S. victims of kidney disease, regardless of ability to pay. Kidney dialysis or transplants become available at no personal cost. The end-stage renal dialysis program now costs approximately ten times the original estimates. Critics question why the government should support treatment for renal failure but not for other similar medical conditions. There is still no national health policy that sets such priorities or clarifies ethical values.

Amendments to the Social Security Act create professional standards review organizations (PSROs) to assure the quality and necessity of care provided to Medicare and Medicaid beneficiaries. This attempt to control costs is controversial, with many physicians viewing it as a federal encroachment on the independent practice of medicine.

1973
The Health Maintenance Organization Act promotes the development of health maintenance organizations (HMOs). An HMO is formed by a group of doctors working together to control costs by offering medical services to individuals and families at a set annual fee. This act successfully encourages the growth of HMOs. They expand from 4 million members in 1973 to an estimated 28 million by 1987; however, their rate of growth begins to slow down by 1988. Although touted during the Reagan era as the answer to rising costs, HMOs have not conclusively been proven to be more efficient, to provide higher quality care, to improve access, or to generate greater patient satisfaction than more traditional forms of health care delivery.

1974
The National Health Planning and Resources Development Act attempts to curtail costs by requiring hospitals and nursing homes to show that they have a definite need to build new facilities or buy new equipment. Critics claim that this and other governmental efforts to control costs are self-defeating in the long run because they create expensive paperwork for participants.

The Employee Retirement Income Security Act (ERISA) provides an exemption from state-mandated benefits for self-insured health and health-related programs. This legislation encourages employers to become self-insured.

1975–
1976 Legislatures of 49 states respond to the malpractice insurance crisis by enacting over 250 pieces of legislation, many of which guarantee the availability of insurance. Some states initiate joint underwriting associations that pool all companies selling liability insurance, while others set an absolute limit on recovery. Much of this legislation will later be struck down in the courts or will fail because of inadequate funding. Most of it fails to successfully address the tort crisis, which will persist through the 1990s.

1976 Amendments to the Health Professions Educational Assistance Act tie medical school subsidies to a requirement that a percentage of residents complete training in general internal medicine, pediatrics, and family medicine. This legislation is an attempt to address the need for primary-care physicians.

The case of Karen Ann Quinlan symbolizes the ethical questions surrounding a comatose patient's right to live or die. The courts refuse her parents' request to remove her from life-support systems until the New Jersey Supreme Court reverses the lower court's decision and grants the request. Ironically, after her respirator is disconnected, Karen lives for nine more years, sustained by tube feeding. The problem does not abate. By 1990, 10,000 people in the United States are in permanently unconscious conditions, maintained by tube feeding.

1978 *In vitro* fertilization leads to the first birth of a normal child by this means. This "test-tube baby" results from the fertilization of a human egg outside its mother's body. After fertilization occurs, the embryo is implanted in the womb. This new procedure raises a host of ethical, legal, and social implications.

1979 A report by the Graduate Medical Education National Advisory Committee predicts a surplus of physicians by 1990. This committee, created by Congress to advise the Department of Health, Education, and Welfare (HEW) on physician manpower issues, also predicts a substantial imbalance in some medical specialties and a marked unevenness in the geographic distribution of physicians. Many predictions of the report turn out to be accurate. The failure of the government to react appropriately to the warning reflects the complexity and overlapping jurisdictions in the U.S. health care system. No single authority sets policy or makes decisions about health care in our pluralistic society.

The surgeon general's report entitled "Healthy People" concludes that the foremost causes of illness lie in individual

1979
cont.
behavior and can be eliminated most effectively through extensive changes in the life-styles of most people. Following the suggestions of this report could save billions of dollars a year; however, no governmental entity has the authority to enforce the report's recommendations. The likelihood of legislating what people eat, how much they exercise, whether they drink alcohol or smoke, or other life-style decisions seems remote in a society that values individualism and freedom of choice.

1970s– 1990s
Increasingly high awards in medical malpractice suits lead to extremely high insurance rates for physicians, especially surgeons and obstetricians. Patients and/or their insurers pay higher costs as a result. Physicians are often forced to practice defensive medicine by ordering more tests and procedures than they would otherwise, to protect themselves in the event of a lawsuit.

1980
Eradication of smallpox worldwide is announced by the World Health Organization. After the discovery of a vaccine for smallpox in 1796, the disease that once killed millions is gradually eradicated from the earth. It is the only disease medical science has completely eliminated. The eradication of smallpox reinforces the rising expectations of the public about the miracles of modern medicine.

An automatic implantable cardioverter and defibrillator (AICD) to prevent cardiac arrest is implanted for the first time in a human heart. This device automatically restores a normal heart rhythm by giving the heart a jolt of electricity. By the mid-1980s, this device, coronary bypass surgery, and other techniques are saving over a third of a million lives a year, but at an enormous cost.

1981
The Omnibus Reconciliation Act phases in cutbacks in federal Medicaid payments to states. These reductions, reaching 4.5 percent in fiscal year 1984, significantly worsen the budgetary problems states are already experiencing with their Medicaid programs. The dual consequences are benefit limitations and tightening of eligibility requirements.

1982
Medicare legislation expands to include the coverage of hospice care, which provides medical and emotional support for patients who choose to die in their own homes. Since hospice care is different from and much cheaper than hospitalization for acute care, this legislation is an attempt to curtail rising costs.

1982
cont.

Scientists create "super mice" by injecting a rat growth hormone gene into fertilized mouse eggs. The technology in this and other experiments, such as those using recombinant DNA techniques, raises a host of ethical questions about genetic engineering.

Barney Clark receives the first artificial heart implant at the University of Utah Medical Center. Although he never leaves the hospital, he survives four months. This operation raises ethical questions about the value of prolonging life if the quality of life is minimal. Critics question how the expense of such an operation can be justified and ask whether physicians could not best use their skills on other procedures.

Charlie Brooks, Jr., a convicted murderer in Texas, is the first person in the United States executed by lethal injection. Although challenged 18 months later in the Supreme Court, the ruling of the lower court is upheld. Lethal injection is still legal, but it poses ethical problems for the physician in attendance. This procedure is in direct violation of the physician's sworn obligation to save lives.

"Baby Doe" is born with Down's syndrome and an incomplete esophagus. His parents refuse to consent to an operation to save the baby's life. In a historical move, the hospital takes the case to the Indiana Supreme Court, which upholds the parents' decision to withhold surgery. The baby dies the following day.

1983

Legislation to curtail the cost of Medicare introduces the concept of diagnosis-related groups (DRGs) by establishing a set of categories based on patient diagnosis, procedures, and age. These categories set standardized reimbursement schedules for hospitals. Although DRGs do reduce costs, critics claim that their use leads to ethically inappropriate practices by hospitals motivated by a desire to increase profits. The prospective-payment system encourages hospitals to discharge patients too early or transfer them to other hospitals.

"Baby Jane Doe" is born with spina bifida and an abnormally small head with excess fluid on the brain. Surgery might prolong her life, but with the support of their physicians, her parents decide not to operate. A right-to-life advocate demands a court review of the decision to forgo surgery, but New York appellate courts throw out his case. The New York State Supreme Court upholds the parents' decision to refuse consent for surgery. The Justice Department becomes involved, and the

1983
cont. case goes all the way to the U.S. Supreme Court, which upholds the state court's ruling in favor of the parents' decision. After six months in the hospital, the child is released and one year later is reported to be alive but severely handicapped.

The family of an 11-month-old girl awaiting a liver transplant in Texas seeks assistance from President Reagan, who appeals for help on national television. A donor is found, but the Texas Medicaid program does not pay for liver transplants. The Texas legislature passes a special bill authorizing payment for just this one transplant and no other. This case is an ethical landmark, posing the question whether access to a life-saving procedure should be based on political clout and publicity.

The President's Commission for the Study of Ethical and Legal Problems in Medicine and Biomedical and Behavioral Research makes major recommendations. Among other things, the commission concludes that society has an ethical obligation to ensure equitable access to health care for all, and that the cost of securing that health care ought to be shared fairly. Although widely well received, this part of the study does not have any direct impact on public policy. The subject of a national health insurance plan has been extremely controversial in the United States for decades. The study also addresses a number of critical ethical questions and proposes a model Uniform Determination of Death Act, which defines death as the irreversible cessation of circulatory and respiratory functions or the irreversible cessation of all functions of the entire brain. By 1988, more than 40 states change their legal standard of death to include brain death.

1984 Responding to the furor over the "Baby Doe" cases, Congress passes the Child Abuse Amendments of 1984. These amendments attempt to redefine child abuse and neglect by expanding neglect to include "the failure to respond to an infant's life-threatening conditions by providing treatment." In 1986, the Supreme Court rules that these so-called Baby Doe regulations are not authorized under the Rehabilitation Act of 1973. The Court stipulates that parents should be the primary decision makers for their children, provided those decisions are in the best interests of the children. The Court emphasizes that child protection is a *state,* not a federal, responsibility.

In a landmark decision, the Florida legislature passes the Winn-Dixie exemption, which automatically licenses doctors who are associated with large HMOs. This circumvention of the

1984
cont.
traditional difficult licensing exam so infuriates physicians already in the state that the following year the Union of American Physicians and Dentists is formed. The state remains a highly competitive medical arena due to the high concentration of elderly patients eligible for Medicare benefits.

The Drug Price Competition and Patent Term Restoration Act results in a major increase in the sale of generic drugs, which becomes a $5 billion industry in five years. With prescription drug prices rising at an average of 10 percent a year since 1980, this is one of many attempts to contain costs. Major pharmaceutical companies complain that legalizing generic drugs is unfair because generic producers do not have to recoup the money spent on researching and developing a product.

"Baby Fae" survives three weeks with a transplanted baboon heart. This California case of experimental surgery fuels the national debate over medical ethics.

The National Organ Transplant Act bans all sales of body organs in response to the commercial selling of organs, such as those perpetrated by the International Kidney Exchange founded several years earlier in Virginia.

A Harvard study estimates that 10 percent of total annual health care costs, or $42 billion a year, is motivated by defensive medical tactics, such as ordering extensive tests, procedures, and return visits that may not be necessary. This practice is a result of the rising incidence of malpractice litigation, which increases physicians' fear of being sued.

Scientists identify the virus that causes AIDS. Fewer than 4,500 Americans have been stricken by the new disease since it was first reported in 1979. However, by 1989, predictions of a dangerous epidemic come true, with a total of over 130,000 reported cases. Public and private resources are increasingly strained in their efforts to provide health care for the afflicted. No cure is known for the disease. The United States lacks an appropriate policy for dealing with such an unexpected epidemic. Funding for research gets entangled in political controversy as various lobbying groups vie for funds. Proponents of funding for AIDS research have to compete with older, more well-established causes.

1985
Magnetic resonance imaging (MRI) is developed. Using no x-rays, this diagnostic device employs a huge magnet that shows

1985
cont.
small subtle differences in tissues and allows doctors to see the body on various planes. Extremely expensive to purchase, install, and operate, MRI is an example of high-technology equipment that contributes to an improved quality of life—and to the rising cost of health care.

Congress mandates in its Consolidated Omnibus Budget Reconciliation Act (COBRA) that employers offer discharged workers (and any dependents in the event of the worker's death) the option to convert at the group rate to an individual policy providing the same benefits. The duration of this coverage is 18 months for the employee and 36 months for survivors. This legislation is created in response to public clamor over the rising cost of health insurance.

Congress directs the secretary of the Department of Health and Human Services to revise the payment schedule for Medicare to reflect the disproportionately high share of charity care provided by a small portion of the nation's hospitals. This move is a recognition that certain teaching hospitals and inner-city hospitals care for a much higher percentage of patients who are unable to pay for their care.

Seventy-six-year-old Roswell Gilbert is sentenced to 25 years in a Florida prison for the mercy killing of his critically ill wife. His sentence is unusually severe. Many perpetrators of mercy killings receive suspended sentences or are asked to do community service. This wide range of judicial response to ethical dilemmas leaves the U.S. public without a clear set of values. In 1989, for example, first-degree murder charges against Rudy Linares are dropped; he had unplugged the life-support system on his comatose and irreversibly brain-damaged 16-month-old son.

The issue over whether not-for-profit hospitals should pay taxes comes to a head in *Utah County v. Intermountain Health Care, Inc.* The Utah Supreme Court rules that hospitals should be exempt from county property taxes only if they are able to satisfy a test relating to "charitable purpose." Criteria for fitting that definition include providing significant services to others without immediate expectation of material reward and support by philanthropy. The controversy over the right to tax-exempt status for not-for-profit hospitals and other health care organizations continues into the 1990s.

Congress creates a Biomedical Ethics Board through the Health Research Extension Act. Composed of six senators and six

1985
cont.
representatives, with an equal number of members from each political party, the board also has an advisory committee of experts in law, medicine, and ethics. The 14-member committee is mandated to counsel members of Congress on ethical issues arising in the delivery of health care and in biomedical research.

1986
Blue Cross/Blue Shield loses federal tax-exempt status nationwide. The U.S. General Accounting Office rules that exemption from federal income taxes gives Blue Cross/Blue Shield an unfair competitive advantage over taxable insurance firms that provide essentially the same services. With the shifts in tax status and more and more large companies turning to self-insurance, major insurance companies are increasingly in fiscal crisis.

Through the Institute of Medicine, Congress establishes the Council on Health Care Technology to promote the development and application of appropriate health care technology assessments. This is another of many government attempts to cut costs and assure quality; however, the council has no clout to enforce its findings.

Congress passes legislation that reduces Medicare payments for graduate medical education. At the same time, many states increase the tuition in medical schools. As a result, 82 percent of medical school graduates incur debts amounting on the average to $33,500.

The American Medical Association's Council on Ethical and Judicial Affairs issues bold new guidelines for doctors in dealing with a family's request to end all treatment involving nutrition and hydration. The guidelines state that it is not unethical to discontinue all means of life-prolonging medical treatment if the patient's coma is irreversible beyond doubt. The following year, the Hastings Center, an institution devoted to the study of medical ethics, publishes similar guidelines that also affirm the right of the individual to refuse any life-sustaining treatment.

Congress passes a law that forbids hospitals to turn away poor patients at emergency rooms before they are "stabilized." For the increasing numbers of indigent and uninsured Americans, the hospital emergency room becomes the primary source of health care services. Inadequate access to high-quality patient care for the poor and the near poor becomes a major component of the health care crisis.

1986
cont.   The Budget Reconciliation Amendment allows hospitals with a disproportionate share of Medicaid patients to receive as much as a 15 percent add-on to their DRG payment levels.

1987   The decision in the "Baby M" case is a landmark in surrogate child custody. In this widely publicized case, Elizabeth and William Stern hire Mary Beth Whitehead to bear their child. They pay her $10,000 and agree to pay her medical expenses. She is artificially inseminated with Mr. Stern's sperm. After the baby's birth on 27 March 1986, Mrs. Whitehead decides to keep the child and forfeits the fee. A court battle ensues, with a New Jersey Superior Court judge enforcing the surrogate agreement and giving William Stern custody of the child. Later, a New Jersey Supreme Court decision reinstates the surrogate mother's right to visit her daughter, which she retains today. This is one of numerous examples of the ethical questions arising from new medical technologies.

Mevacor is introduced to reduce cholesterol. The cost of testing drugs is high, but pharmaceutical companies with successful new drugs have the potential to make large profits in an increasingly competitive market. Critics claim that federal regulations are too steep, which drives up the cost of new drugs; opponents say that regulations are not steep enough. In either case, consumers and insurers help pay the bill for pharmaceutical research.

1988   Oregon passes a law that stops Medicaid funding for most organ transplants and expands prenatal-care services instead. Averaging more than $150,000 per procedure for a projected 30 recipients a year, heart, liver, bone marrow, and pancreas transplants are deemed unaffordable. Oregon's legislature is currently considering a bill to ration all health care covered by Medicaid. Other states are watching to see what will happen if and when this legislation ends up in the courts.

The federal government drops funding for the development of artificial human hearts. Cost containment in health care becomes an increasing concern of the government.

1989   Ruling in the "right to die" case of *Cruzan v. Director of Missouri Department of Health,* the U.S. Supreme Court says that states are justified in requiring "clear and convincing" evidence of the wishes of comatose patients before allowing withdrawal of life-sustaining treatment. This ruling denies the request of the parents of 32-year-old Nancy Cruzan to discontinue artificial

1989
cont.
nutrition and hydration of their daughter, who has been in a severely and irreversibly brain-damaged state since a 1983 car accident. After the Supreme Court ruling, the Missouri court hears new evidence that recounts specific conversations in which Nancy stated that she would not want to be kept alive in an irreversible coma. The Missouri court reverses its decision, and the feeding tube is withdrawn. Nancy Cruzan dies two weeks later on 26 December 1990. After the U.S. Supreme Court decision, right-to-life advocates report that inquiries about living wills increase 500-fold.

The Florida Birth-Related Neurological Injury Compensation Plan goes into effect. This no-fault program, funded by assessments on participating physicians and hospitals, offers structured compensation to cover costs of present and future care if an infant's problem is neurological and related to a problem at birth. Parents can receive no more than an additional $100,000 for noneconomic damages.

1980s
Intraocular lens implants become one of the most popular operations of the decade. Performed on half a million Americans annually, the operation to remove a cataract and implant a lens takes less than one hour. Costs to insurers rise as the public clamors for a procedure that was once unavailable. Critics claim that as long as the majority of Americans do not pay directly for health care, the demand for expensive procedures will continue to escalate. Companies that have instituted higher copayment policies for employees covered by health insurance find that usage rates decrease.

1990
The U.S. Bipartisan Commission on Comprehensive Health Care (the Pepper Commission) proposes universal health insurance to Congress. This plan would require all employers to provide health insurance coverage to their workers and dependents or pay a payroll tax toward coverage under a public plan. Smaller employers would also be given tax credits for the purchase of private health insurance. Medicaid would be abolished, and the poor and near poor would be covered under a uniform national public plan with federal and state tax financing. The controversial plan is criticized for failing to contain health care costs and to identify necessary revenues to implement the plan.

Congress passes a law requiring drug companies to give Medicaid the same deep discounts they give other big customers. But instead of reducing Medicaid drug prices, many pharmaceutical

1990
cont.
companies raise prices to their other large customers. Like many cost-containment measures, this legislation leads to cost shifting. Consumers, and ultimately insurance companies, will pay for the increased cost of drugs.

3

Biographies

THE FOLLOWING ARE BRIEF BIOGRAPHICAL SKETCHES of individuals who play or have played key roles in addressing the health care crisis in the United States. They include researchers, theorists, authors, politicians, physicians, and leaders in major organizations. They also include people who, by virtue of their positions, are likely to have a significant effect on the current and future direction of health care in the United States.

Like all such lists, this one is necessarily subjective and incomplete. Many unmentioned researchers, writers, spokespersons, program directors, health care professionals, and volunteers have contributed their time and energy to efforts to better understand, and to solve, the current health care crisis. The people cited here are representative of that greater whole.

Morris B. Abram (1918–)

Morris B. Abram served as chairman of the President's Commission for the Study of Ethical and Legal Problems in Medicine and Biomedical and Behavioral Research in 1983. A retired New York attorney now serving as the U.S. ambassador to Switzerland, Abram is the former president of Brandeis University and an advocate of human and civil rights. He has served previously at the behest of U.S. presidents in various capacities. President John F. Kennedy appointed him as first general counsel to the Peace Corps in 1961, and President Lyndon B. Johnson named him to serve as the U.S. representative to the United Nations

Commission on Human Rights between 1965 and 1968. He frequently lectures before professional organizations throughout the United States and abroad on the subjects of biomedical ethics and civil rights.

Abram has served as a member of the Mt. Sinai Hospital Human Subjects Review Panel and as a member of the U.S. Subcommission on Prevention of Discrimination and Protection of Minorities. He is a long-time chairman of the United Negro College Fund and has served as president of the American Jewish Committee. A former Rhodes scholar, he graduated from the University of Chicago Law School in 1940. He is listed in *Who's Who in America.*

Drew E. Altman (1951–)

A widely known foundation and public policy expert in the fields of health and human services, Drew E. Altman is the president of the Henry J. Kaiser Family Foundation, one of the nation's largest and most active foundations in the field of health. Altman, who received a Ph.D. in political science from the Massachusetts Institute of Technology in 1983, was formerly director of the health and human services program of the Pew Charitable Trusts in Philadelphia. As commissioner of the Department of Human Services for the state of New Jersey from 1986 to 1989, he designed and implemented a welfare reform program in New Jersey. As vice-president of the Robert Wood Johnson Foundation from 1981 to 1986, he designed several national programs in health care financing and cost containment, health insurance for the poor, prepaid managed health care, health care for the homeless, and programs for people with AIDS. Prior to joining the Johnson Foundation, he was special assistant, Office of the Administrator, in the Health Care Financing Administration of the U.S. Department of Health and Human Services. He has held appointments as senior research associate and lecturer at Brandeis and at M.I.T. He has published numerous journal articles on health and human services issues.

Stuart H. Altman (1937–)

Stuart H. Altman is dean of the Heller Graduate School for Social Policy, Brandeis University, and Sol C. Chaikin professor of national health policy. He is in his second term as chairman of the congressionally legislated Prospective Payment Assessment Commission, which is responsible for overseeing the Medicare DRG hospital payment system. Between 1971 and 1976, Altman was deputy assistant secretary for planning and evaluation/health at the Department of Health, Education, and Welfare. While serving in that position, he was one of the principal contributors to the development and advancement of the administration's national health insurance proposal. From 1973 to 1974, he served as deputy director for health on the President's Cost-of-Living Council, where he was responsible for developing the council's program on health care cost containment. Altman has served as a member of the board of the Robert Wood Johnson Clinical Scholars Program and on the governing council of the Institute of Medicine. He is listed in *Who's Who in America.*

Altman received a Ph.D. in economics in 1964 from the University of California, Los Angeles, and has taught at Brown University and the University of California, Berkeley. He serves on the editorial boards of several publications, including *Health Policy.* He is the coauthor of *Federal Health Policy: Problems and Prospects* (1981), *Ambulatory Care: Problems of Cost and Access* (1983), and *Competition and Compassion: Conflicting Roles for Public Hospitals* (1989), plus other books and numerous journal articles.

Tom L. Beauchamp (1939–)

Tom L. Beauchamp is a professor of philosophy and senior research scholar at the Kennedy Institute of Ethics at Georgetown University in Washington, D.C., where he has been on the faculty since 1970. He served as a staff philosopher for the National Committee on Protection of Human Subjects of Biomedical and Behavioral Research at the National Institutes of Health from 1977 to 1979. He has served in numerous professional positions, including chairman of the Committee on Medicine and Philosophy of the American Philosophical Association from 1985 to 1988. He has served as a consultant on medical ethics to numerous federal agencies, hospitals, law firms, physician groups, and nursing groups. In addition, he was an advisory board member for the National Public Radio and Educational Television series, "Ethics in America." Beauchamp has edited numerous publications in the medical ethics field and serves as editorial board member of *Ethics, Journal of Business Ethics,* and *Journal of Medicine and Philosophy.* He is listed in *Who's Who in America.* His writings include *Principles of Biomedical Ethics* (1979) and *Medical Ethics* (1984) as well as numerous articles in professional journals.

Beauchamp received a Ph.D. in philosophy from Johns Hopkins University in 1970. His current research includes ethical issues in the prevention of AIDS infection.

Robert J. Blendon (1942–)

Robert J. Blendon is professor and chairman of the Department of Health Policy and Management of the Harvard University School of Public Health. In addition, this prominent participant in the national health care scene serves as deputy director of the Harvard University Division of Health Policy Research and Education. Prior to his Harvard appointment in 1987, Blendon was senior vice-president at the Robert Wood Johnson Foundation, where he worked for 15 years. In addition to serving as special assistant to the undersecretary of the Department for Policy Development in the Department of Health, Education, and Welfare, Blendon has held appointments at Princeton University and the Johns Hopkins University Schools of Medicine and Public Health. He is best known for his research on access to health care, private giving in health, AIDS and discrimination, medicine in China, and public opinion on health care.

Blendon holds a doctoral degree from the School of Public Health of Johns Hopkins University, where his principal attention was directed toward health services administration and public policy. He has served in various capacities, including as adviser to the secretary of the treasury on private philanthropy and public needs. He is a member of the Institute of Medicine of the National Academy of Sciences and serves on the editorial board of the *Journal of the American Medical Association (JAMA).* He is president of the Association for Health Services Research, chairman of the Institute of Medicine's Committee on Access to Health Care, and a participant in numerous other boards and organizations. Among Blendon's many honors are inclusion in *American Men and Women of Science, Distinguished Leaders in Health Care,* and *Who's Who in America.* He has authored numerous articles in prestigious journals such as *JAMA, New England Journal of Medicine,* and *Health Affairs.*

Robert Henry Brook (1943–)

A physician, educator, and health services researcher, Robert Henry Brook is chief of the division of geriatrics and professor of both medicine and public health at UCLA. He is also director of the health sciences program at Rand Corporation. He serves on the editorial board for numerous publications, including the *Health Administration Press,* the *Journal of General Internal Medicine, Health Policy,* and *Health Week.* A frequent public speaker, Brook is the recipient of numerous honors and awards. He received the Baxter Health Services Research Prize in 1988 and served as a member of the advisory panel for the Office of Technology Assessment study, "The Quality of Medical Care."

Brook received an M.D. from the Johns Hopkins Medical School in 1968 and an Sc.D. degree from the Johns Hopkins School of Hygiene and Public Health in 1972. In 1990, he was elected into the Johns Hopkins Society of Scholars. He is a reviewer for numerous prestigious magazines and a member of many organizations, including the American Association of Physicians, the American Society for Clinical Investigation, the Institute of Medicine, and the American College of Physicians. He is listed in *Who's Who in America.* Brook is the coauthor of *Appropriateness of Use of Selected Medical and Surgical Procedures and Its Relationship to Geographic Variations in Their Use (1989)* and *Changing Medical Practice through Technology Assessment: An Evaluation of the NIH Consensus Development Program* (1989). He has also written numerous journal articles, book chapters, and research reports.

Joseph A. Califano, Jr. (1931–)

Former secretary of health, education, and welfare, Joseph A. Califano, Jr., is currently practicing law with a firm in Washington, D.C., and is admitted to practice before the Supreme Court. During his tenure as secretary from 1977 to 1979, Califano undertook a complete reorganization of the department; in addition, the first surgeon general's report on health promotion and disease prevention was issued, and the department instituted computerized techniques to oversee welfare, Medicare, and Medicaid programs. Numerous other changes took place, including the issuance of regulations to provide equal opportunities to the handicapped and the aged. The secretary took special interest in cost-containment efforts regarding health care.

A graduate of Harvard Law School in 1955, Califano has served in numerous capacities in the government. An expert in health care delivery and cost containment, he consults and lectures widely about the U.S. health care system and is a member of the Institute of Medicine of the National Academy of Sciences. Among his many directorships are those with Chrysler Corporation; Primerica Corporation; Automatic Data Processing, Inc.; K mart; Georgetown University; and Friends of the National Library of Medicine. He has received honorary degrees from numerous colleges and universities and is listed in *Who's Who in America*. His health care publications include *The 1982 Report on Drug Abuse and Alcoholism* (1982) and *America's Health Care Revolution: Who Lives? Who Dies?* (1986). He has also published articles in *The New York Times, The Washington Post, Reader's Digest,* and *New Republic*.

Daniel Callahan (1930–)

Daniel Callahan is director of the Hastings Center, a think tank in Briarcliff Manor, New York, which he helped found 22 years ago. Called "the nation's leading medical ethicist" by *Time*, Callahan is best known for his opinion that health care for the aged should be limited. He believes that resources spent on the long-term treatment of the elderly could be better utilized, pointing out that chronic care is draining funds from the health needs of other groups and from urgent social problems, such as education.

Callahan earned a Ph.D. in philosophy from Harvard in 1965 and cofounded the Hastings Center with psychiatrist Willard Gaylin in 1969. The nonprofit center has 12 professionals and a support staff of 15 and runs on an annual budget of $1.6 million. Hastings ethicists are regularly called upon to consult in controversial ethics cases. They also publish regularly, draw up model legislation, and develop guidelines for public policy. Callahan has personally served as principal investigator for at least one major research project each year for 20 years. He lectures widely and has served as a visiting professor in several universities.

Callahan's numerous professional activities include serving as a special consultant on the Presidential Commission on

Population Growth and the American Future, on the advisory panel for the Project on Life-Sustaining Technologies and the Elderly for the U.S. Congress, and on the advisory council for Americans for Generational Equity. He has received numerous awards, including the 1988 Pulitzer Prize for nonfiction for his book, *Setting Limits: Medical Goals in an Aging Society*. His other publications include *What Kind of Life: The Limits of Medical Progress* (1990) plus numerous project reports, essays, and articles. He is listed in *Who's Who in America*, *Who's Who in Health Care*, *Directory of American Scholars*, *American Men and Women of Science*, and *Contemporary Authors*.

Wilbur J. Cohen (1913–1987)

Wilbur J. Cohen has been called the "father of the Social Security System." In 1936, he was director of the cabinet-level Committee on Economic Security, whose report formed the basis of the Social Security Act. After the act was passed, Cohen joined the staff of the Social Security Administration as technical adviser to the commissioner. He worked there from 1936 to 1955, and at the time of his resignation he was director of the Division of Research and Statistics.

Cohen's interest in health care stretched throughout a career that began in 1934 and continued until the day he died. He wrote the original memo on Medicare as the technical adviser to the commissioner of Social Security in 1950 and served as technical adviser in the drafting and passage of the Kerr-Mills amendment in 1960. He managed the legislative and technical processes, under the direct supervision of Presidents Kennedy and Johnson, that led to the passage of Medicare/Medicaid legislation in 1965. Between 1961 and 1969, Cohen helped to formulate nearly all of the nation's health care legislation. This process began in 1961 when he became assistant secretary for legislation at the Department of Health, Education, and Welfare (HEW), and continued in 1965 when President Johnson appointed him undersecretary of HEW. In 1968 he became secretary of HEW.

During his long public career, Cohen received innumerable citations, awards, and honorary degrees, including the Rockefeller Public Service Award in 1967. Cohen graduated from the University of Wisconsin with an undergraduate degree in economics in 1934. He was the author of several books and numerous articles on health care in the popular press. From 1956 to 1965, he was the principal author of most of the articles that appeared in the *Social Security Bulletin*.

Karen Davis (1942–)

Karen Davis chairs the Department of Health Policy and Management in the School of Hygiene and Public Health and has a joint appointment as professor of economics at Johns Hopkins University. She was formerly a senior fellow at the Brookings Institution and served as deputy assistant secretary for planning and evaluation/health at the U.S. Department of Health and Human Services and as administrator of the Public Health Service for the Health Resources Administration. Her specialty is health policy analysis and legislation. Her current research interests include acute and long-term care for the elderly, physician supply and distribution, access to health care, child health, health care costs, and design of innovative provider reimbursement methods.

Davis is director of the Commonwealth Fund Commission on Elderly People Living Alone. She is a member of the Physician Payment Review Commission, the Institute of Medicine of the National Academy of Sciences, and the Maryland Governor's Commission on Health Care Policy and Financing. She also sits on several boards and committees concerned with health policy issues and serves on the editorial board of several professional journals.

Davis received a Ph.D. in economics from Rice University in 1969. She is listed in *Who's Who in America*. Her publications include *National Health Insurance: Benefits, Costs, and Consequences* (1975), *Health and the War on Poverty: A Ten Year Appraisal* (1978), *Medicare Policy: New Directions for Health and Long-Term Care* (1986), *Health Care Cost Containment* (1990), and numerous other books and articles on health economics and policy analysis.

Barbara A. Donaho (1933–)

Barbara A. Donaho is the senior vice-president of patient services at St. Anthony's Hospital in St. Petersburg, Florida. She previously held executive-level positions in Shands Hospital at the University of Florida and the Sisters of Mercy Health Corporation. Recently completing a term as a member of the American Hospital Association board of directors, she received its Trustees Award in 1988. Since 1979, she has served as commissioner of the

Joint Commission on Accreditation of Hospitals and was the first nurse to be appointed to that position. She chaired the accreditation committee from 1983 to 1987. She has also chaired the American Hospital Association's Council on Nursing and is past president of the Midwest Alliance in Nursing and the American Organization of Nurse Executives. She has served on numerous boards, advisory panels, and committees, including the Healthcare Cost Containment Board, the National Commission on Nursing Implementation Project Task Force, and the advisory panel on nursing education/nursing service for the Institute of Medicine of the National Academy of Sciences.

Donaho received a B.S.N. degree from Johns Hopkins University in 1956 and an M.A. from the University of Chicago in 1958. She has held faculty appointments at the University of Florida, the University of Michigan, the University of Minnesota, and Boston University. She has been listed in *Who's Who in American Women* and serves on the editorial boards of numerous journals, including *Nursing Economics* and *Nursing Outlook*. She has published many professional papers and journal articles.

Robert Higgins Ebert (1914–)

The retired dean of the medical school at Harvard University and president of Harvard Medical Center, Robert Higgins Ebert has had a long, distinguished career as an educator and medical school executive. He was a professor of medicine at the University of Chicago, Western Reserve University, and Harvard. He has received numerous awards, including the Alumni Achievement Medal from the University of Chicago in 1968 and the Distinguished Service Award in 1962. Ebert is a member of numerous professional associations, including the Academy of Arts and Sciences. He served as a trustee for the Rockefeller Foundation and as a member of the National Advisory Committee on Health Manpower. In addition, he has served on the board of regents for the National Library of Medicine, on the advisory committee to the director at the National Institutes of Health, and is still serving as a member of the board of the Harvard Community Health Plan. He is listed in *Who's Who in America*.

Ebert received his M.D. in 1942 from the University of Chicago and a Ph.D. from the University of Oxford in 1939. He has written extensively, focusing primarily on the field of medical education.

David M. Eddy (1941–)

David M. Eddy is professor of health policy and management at Duke University. After serving on the faculty at Stanford as a professor in engineering and medicine, he went to Duke University in 1981 to set up the Center for Health Policy Research and Education. Eddy's research goal has been to develop and apply methods for evaluating health practices and designing practice policies. He has developed policies for a number of organizations, including the American Cancer Society, National Cancer Institute, World Health Organization, the Office of Technology Assessment, the Blue Cross and Blue Shield Association, and the American Medical Association.

Much of Eddy's work is related to cancer. He authored the American Cancer Society's *Guidelines on Cancer Screening* in 1980; his mathematical model of cancer screening was awarded the 1980 Lanchester Prize, the top award in the field of operations research. His follow-up article in the *Journal of the American Medical Association* created a controversy when he questioned the cost-effectiveness of widespread mammography. His recent work has focused on methods for estimating the outcomes of health practices and designing practice policies. He has developed a computer model for planning national cancer control programs.

Eddy received an M.D. from the University of Virginia in 1964 and a Ph.D. in engineering economic systems from Stanford in 1978. He serves on the board of mathematics of the National Academy of Sciences and is a member of the Institute of Medicine of the National Academy of Sciences.

Alain Enthoven (1930–)

Described by *Business and Health* as "one of the leading members of the country's informal and exclusive health care policy brain trust," Alain Enthoven is a well-known proponent of universal health coverage. Currently a professor of public and private management at the Graduate School of Business and professor of health research at Stanford University, Enthoven has worked for Rand Corporation, consulted for the Brookings Institution, served as assistant secretary for systems analysis at the Department of Defense, and was president of Litton Medical Products. His major research interest is economics and public policy in health care. Three bills that have been introduced into Congress were based on the principles of his health care plan. He has served as a consultant to the Kaiser Foundation health plan and sits on the Health Benefits Advisory Council for the Public Employees Retirement System of California.

Enthoven received a Ph.D. in economics from the Massachusetts Institute of Technology in 1956 and is the recipient of numerous awards, including the President's Award for Distinguished Federal Civilian Service and the Department of Defense Medal for Distinguished Public Service. He is a Rhodes scholar, a fellow of the American Academy of Arts and Sciences, and is listed in *Who's Who in America*. His publications include *Health Plan: The Only Practical Solution to the Soaring Cost of Medical Care* (1980) and numerous journal articles. An updated version of his health plan proposal was published in the 5 and 12 January 1989 issues of the *New England Journal of Medicine*.

Martin S. Feldstein (1939–)

An economist and educator with special interest in health care economics, Martin S. Feldstein has served as a professor of economics at Harvard University since 1969. He is president of the National Bureau of Economic Research and was chairman of the Council of Economic Advisers from 1982 to 1984. He was also on the faculty of Oxford University.

Feldstein earned a Ph.D. from Oxford University in 1967. He has served as consultant and adviser to numerous corporations and institutions, including Hospital Corporation of America, Dean Witter Reynolds, and Data Resources, Inc. He received the John Bates Clark Medal from the American Economic Association in 1977 and is a member of the Institute of Medicine of the National Academy of Sciences. Feldstein is listed in *Who's Who in America*. His publications include numerous scientific papers, and he has been the editor of several books.

Carl L. Figliola

A professor of health care and public administration at C. W. Post Center of Long Island University, Carl L. Figliola has served as dean of the school of health and public service since 1981. He has been active in the American Society for Public Administration, the National Association of Schools of Public Affairs and Administration, and the New York State Public Health

Association, Long Island Region. Figliola has been a leader in professional education and developed the first M.P.A. degree programs in health care and public administration on Long Island. A member of various boards and task forces, he has also been a consultant to government and to health care facilities. He received his Ph.D. from New York University. Publications include articles in the field of management and public policy.

Willard Gaylin (1925–)

Willard Gaylin is clinical professor of psychiatry at Columbia College of Physicians and Surgeons and also practices psychiatry and psychoanalysis privately. He was cofounder of the Hastings Center, which researches ethical issues in the life sciences. He has been the center's president since its inception in 1969. This noted medical ethicist and author maintains that biotechnology has "medicalized" society to the extent that most people expect a treatment or cure for every ailment and seldom consider the cost. He predicts that as technology becomes rationed, the curing role of the medical profession will return to the caring emphasis of the past.

Gaylin has been elected a member of the Institute of Medicine, a fellow of the American Psychiatric Association, and a fellow of the New York Psychiatric Society. He has received the George E. Daniels Medal for contributions to psychoanalytic medicine, the Van Gieson Award for outstanding contributions to the mental health sciences, and has held various visiting lecturer positions. He presently serves on the boards of directors of the Planned Parenthood Federation of America, Helsinki Watch, and Medical/Scientific Board of the National Aphasia Association and is past chairman of the Human Rights Task Force of the American Psychiatric Association. The 1981 KCTS/TV series, "Hard Choices," for which he was the narrator, received an Alfred I. DuPont/Columbia Broadcast Award for excellence in TV journalism. Gaylin is listed in *Who's Who in America*.

Gaylin received his M.D. from Western Reserve Medical School in 1951 and a Certificate in Psychoanalytic Education from the Columbia Psychoanalytic School in 1956. His publications include *Doing Good: The Limits of Benevolence* (1978), *Feelings: Our Vital Signs* (1979), *The Killing of Bonnie Garland: A Question of Justice* (1982), *The Rage Within: Anger in Modern Life* (1984),

Rediscovering Love (1986), and *Adam and Eve and Pinocchio: On Being and Becoming Human* (1990).

Eli Ginzberg (1911–)

Eli Ginzberg has served on the faculty of Columbia University in various capacities since 1935 and is currently professor emeritus in the Graduate School of Business. He also served as adjunct professor of health and society at Barnard College from 1980 to 1988. Ginzberg is an economist, government consultant, and author. Some of his many appointments to government advisory positions have been directly related to health care. He has served, for example, as director of a New York State hospital study, as an adviser to the Committee on Chronic Illness, as a member of the advisory council to the National Institute of Mental Health, and as a national adviser on the Allied Health Council.

Ginzberg received a Ph.D. from Columbia University in 1934. He has been the recipient of many awards, including a medal from the War Department for exceptional civilian service and the National Health Achievement Award in Health Economics, presented by the Blue Cross and Blue Shield Association. He has served as consultant to numerous corporations and foundations and is a fellow of the American Association for the Advancement of Science and the American Academy of Arts and Sciences. He is listed in *Who's Who in America*.

Currently working on a comprehensive book on the political economy of health, Ginzberg does not expect any major reform in the U.S. health care system during this decade unless a major financial crisis occurs. Many of Ginzberg's extensive publications are related to health care. Some of his most recent titles include *American Medicine: The Power Shift* (1985), *The U.S. Health Care System: A Look to the 1990s* (1985), *From Health Dollars to Health Services: New York City* (1965–1985, 1986), *Medicine and Society: Clinical Decisions and Societal Values* (1988), *Young People at Risk: Is Prevention Possible?* (1988), *The Financing of Biomedical Research* (1989), and *The Medical Triangle* (1990).

Howard H. Hiatt (1925–)

Howard H. Hiatt has served on the faculty at Harvard University since 1955. Much of his early research focused on the application of advances in molecular biology to medical problems. He was a member of the team that first identified and described messenger RNA. From 1963 to 1972, he was the Herrman L. Blumgart professor of medicine at Harvard Medical School and physician-in-chief at Beth Israel Hospital. From 1972 to 1984, he was dean of the Harvard School of Public Health. Since that time, Hiatt has been professor of medicine in both the Harvard Medical School and the School of Public Health and senior physician at the Brigham and Women's Hospital.

Hiatt is the principal investigator for the Harvard Medical Practice Study, which in 1990 completed a four-year investigation of medical injury, medical malpractice, and the tort litigation system in the state of New York. His present research is also concerned with the social aspects of medicine and health, particularly the effects of poverty on health. He has long been involved in efforts to focus attention on health, particularly that of children, as an issue for bringing people together.

The recipient of numerous honors, Hiatt received an M.D. from Harvard in 1948. He has served on various boards and committees and is a member of the Association of American Physicians, the Institute of Medicine of the National Academy of Sciences, the American Academy of Arts and Sciences, and several other organizations. He is listed in *Who's Who in America*. His publications include *America's Health in the Balance: Choice or Chance* (1987), *Medical Lifeboat: Will There Be Room for You in the Health Care System?* (1989), plus numerous articles in both professional journals and the popular press.

Robert Kane (1940–)

A graduate of Harvard Medical School and board-certified in preventive medicine, Robert Kane is currently chairman of long-term care and aging at the School of Public Health at the University of Minnesota. In addition, Kane has held academic appointments at the University of Utah, the UCLA Schools of Medicine and Public Health, and the USC Leonard Davis School of Gerontology. Formerly a senior researcher at Rand Corporation, he has served as a consultant to numerous organizations, including the National Institute on Aging, the National Center for Health Services Research, the Institute of Medicine, and the World Health Organization. The principal investigator on over 40 research projects, Kane is the recipient of the Geriatric Medicine Academic Award, the American Geriatric Society Edward B.

Henderson Memorial Lecture Award, and the American Public Health Association Gerontological Health Key Award. He is listed in *Who's Who in America.*

Kane has written many books. His most recent titles include *A Will and a Way: What the United States Can Learn about Long-Term Care from Canada* (1985), *Long-Term Care: Principles, Programs and Policies* (1987), *Clinics in Geriatric Medicine* (1989), and *Improving the Health of Older People* (1990). Kane has also published numerous journal articles and research reports and frequently contributes chapters for books on geriatric health care.

Edward Kennedy (1932–)

Long known as a supporter of national health care, Edward Kennedy has served as a U.S. senator from Massachusetts since 1962. He is chairman of the Labor and Human Resources Committee and served as chairman of that committee's subcommittee on health from 1971 to 1980. Currently, Kennedy is sponsoring the Basic Health Benefits for All Americans Act in response to the health care crisis. That bill would extend the current system of employment-based private insurance as well as extend the federal-state Medicaid program to cover uninsured nonworkers and members of their families.

Kennedy serves on numerous other subcommittees and is chairman of the Technology Assessment Board and a member of the Biomedical Ethics Board. A graduate of the University of Virginia Law School in 1959, Kennedy has received many awards, including the Leadership Conference on Civil Rights Hubert H. Humphrey Award for selfless and distinguished service in the cause of equality. He appears on the daily radio program "Face Off" with Senator Alan Simpson. Kennedy is listed in *Who's Who in America.* He wrote *In Critical Condition: The Crisis in America's Health Care* (1972).

William Lee Kissick (1932–)

William Lee Kissick's career in health policy and planning spans 25 years in government and academe. During the Kennedy and Johnson administrations, he held several appointments in the U.S. Public Health Service; Department of Health, Education, and Welfare; and the White House. He is the George Seckel Pepper professor of public health and preventive medicine in the School of Medicine at the University of Pennsylvania, professor of health care systems at Wharton, and director of the Leonard Davis Institute of Health Economics Center for Health Policy and Planning. He is a well-known expert in public health policy, comparative health care systems, and health systems planning.

Kissick has served in a variety of advisory capacities and is currently a councillor for The College of Physicians of Philadelphia, health adviser for the Gray Panthers, and serves on the executive committee of the Philadelphia Chapter of Physicians for Social Responsibility. Kissick received an M.D. in 1957, an M.P.H. (Master of Public Health) in 1959, and a Dr. P.H. (Doctor of Public Health) in 1961, all from Yale University. He is a frequent lecturer and has served widely as a consultant. He has received numerous honors, including the Nobel Peace Prize, which he shared in 1985 with the Physicians for Social Responsibility, U.S. Affiliate of International Physicians for the Prevention of Nuclear War. He received the Distinguished Alumni Award from the Association of Yale Alumni in Medicine and Yale School of Medicine in 1988. He is listed in *Who's Who in America, Who's Who in Health Care, Who's Who in Technology Today,* and *Who's Who in the World.* He is coeditor of *Lessons from the First Twenty Years of Medicare: Research Implications for Public and Private Sector Policy* (1989) and has written numerous other books and journal articles.

Richard D. Lamm (1935–)

The governor of Colorado from 1975 to 1987, Richard D. Lamm is currently director of the Center for Public Policy and Contemporary Issues at the University of Denver. His research and teaching focus has been in the health policy area, with a special emphasis on generational health care issues and the allocation of health care resources. In 1984, he created a national controversy by speaking out about the terminally ill's "duty to die." Although he was quoted out of context, Lamm's stance established him as a forthright advocate of the growing need to make difficult health care decisions. He is one of a new breed of policy analysts who argues that the challenge of the 1990s is to meet new public needs with evermore limited resources.

In addition to teaching and lecturing, Lamm practices law with a private firm in Denver, Colorado. He was selected as one of *Time* magazine's "200 Young Leaders of America" in 1974 and won the *Christian Science Monitor*'s "Peace 2010" essay competition in 1985. He received his LL.B. from the University of California in 1961 and is listed in *Who's Who in America*. Lamm wrote *The Immigration Time Bomb: The Fragmenting of America* (1985) and *Megatraumas: America in the Year 2000* (1985) plus various articles and a syndicated column in the *Rocky Mountain News*.

Mary Lasker

A major philanthropist, health lobbyist, and civic worker, Mary Lasker is cofounder of the Albert and Mary Lasker Foundation. This educational and medical research foundation gives awards for contributions to medical research and public health administration. Lasker has played a key role in encouraging both private and government funding of medical research in the United States. She has served as the guiding force for numerous organizations and is especially well known for her efforts to fight cancer. She is a trustee of Research to Prevent Blindness and is on the board of directors of the executive committee of the American Cancer Society. She is also a member of the executive committee of the National Committee Against Mental Illness, president of the board of the United Cerebral Palsy Research and Educational Foundation, and chairperson of the National Health Education Committee.

Lasker is the recipient of many awards and honorary degrees and is listed in *Who's Who in America*. In 1984, Congress named a new center at the National Institutes of Health in her honor, and in 1989 she received a Congressional Gold Medal for her humanitarian contributions in the areas of medical research, education, urban beautification, and the fine arts. The Mary Woodard Lasker Professorship of Health Sciences was established at the Harvard School of Public Health in 1989. In 1990, she was inducted into the Health Care Hall of Fame.

Kenneth G. Manton (1947–)

Kenneth G. Manton is research professor and research director of demographic studies at Duke University and medical research professor at Duke University Medical Center's Department of Community and Family Medicine. Manton is also a senior fellow of the Duke University Medical Center's Center for the Study of Aging and Human Development and assistant director of the Duke University Center for Demographic Studies. In 1986, he was named head of the World Health Organization Collaborating

Center for Research and Training in Methods of Assessing Risk and Forecasting Health Status Trends as Related to Multiple Disease Outcomes, based at the Center for Demographic Studies. In 1990, Manton was the recipient of the Mindel C. Sheps Award in mathematical demography, presented by the Population Association of America.

Manton is the principal investigator of four major research projects funded by the National Institute on Aging and several other grants and contracts with other federal agencies. His current research interests include forecasting morbidity, disability, and mortality among the nation's elderly; reimbursement maintenance of quality care for both acute- and long-term-care services for the elderly; and mathematical modeling of physiological aging processes of human mortality at advanced ages.

Manton received a Ph.D. in sociology from Duke University in 1974. He frequently gives presentations and is a member of several editorial boards. His publications include *Recent Trends in Mortality Analysis* (1984), *Chronic Disease Risk Modelling: Measurement and Evaluation of the Risks of Chronic Disease Processes* (1988), and several other books, including a forthcoming title through Oxford University Press, *Forecasting the Health of the Old.*

Theodore R. Marmor (1939–)

A professor of public management and political science in the Yale School of Organization of Management and Yale College, Theodore R. Marmor formerly taught political science and public management at the University of Wisconsin, the University of Minnesota, and the University of Chicago. He has served the government in various capacities, including as special assistant to the undersecretary of the Department of Health, Education, and Welfare and appointments to the President's Commission on Income Maintenance Programs and the Presidential Commission on a National Agenda for the 80s. Marmor is currently a fellow of the Canadian Institute for Advanced Research, where he works with colleagues on issues of health policy in advanced industrial nations.

In addition to serving on numerous advisory and editorial boards, Marmor is a founding member of the National Academy for Social Insurance. He writes and lectures frequently about the politics and policies of the welfare state and has received numerous honors and fellowships. In addition, Marmor serves as a member of the advisory board for the Center for National Policy. He has consulted for many well-known organizations, including the Ways and Means Committee of Congress, the Department of Health and Human Services, the National Institutes of Health, the Rand Corporation, and the Ford Foundation.

Marmor received a Ph.D. from Harvard University in 1966 and is listed in *Who's Who in America*. He wrote *The Politics of Medicare* (1970), *National Health Insurance* (1980), *Health Care Policy: A Political Economy Approach* (1982), and *Political Analysis and American Medical Care* (1983) and coauthored *Social Security: Beyond the Rhetoric of Crisis* (1988) and *America's Misunderstood Welfare State: Persistent Myths, Enduring Realities* (1990).

J. Alexander McMahon (1921–)

Currently serving as chairman of the Department of Health Administration at Duke University, J. Alexander McMahon was president of the American Hospital Association from 1972 to 1986. Prior to that, he was president of North Carolina Blue Cross and Blue Shield. He has worked in various other capacities, including vice-president for special development for the Hospital Savings Association in Chapel Hill, general counsel for the North Carolina Association of County Commissioners, and professor of public law and government and assistant director of the Institute of Government at the University of North Carolina.

McMahon is a nationally known speaker on health care issues. He has been active in a number of professional organizations and has served on many boards and commissions related to health care. Some of his most recent contributions include serving as a member of the National Leadership Commission on Health Care, the National Advisory Committee of the Robert Wood Johnson Community Programs for Affordable Health Care, and the Strategy 2000 Policy Advisory Panel for Paralyzed Veterans of America.

McMahon graduated from Harvard Law School in 1984 and holds several honorary degrees. He is the recipient of numerous awards, including the American Society for Healthcare, Human Resources Administration/Hall of Fame Award in 1987. McMahon is listed in *Who's Who in America*. He has written guidebooks and articles on county government and local finance plus numerous journal articles and other publications related to health care.

Walter J. McNerney (1925–)

Walter J. McNerney is the Herman Smith research professor of health policy at the Kellogg Graduate School of Management and chairman of Walter J. McNerney and Associates, a management consulting firm in the health care field. After five years as a teacher of hospital administration at the University of Pittsburgh and administrator of one of the medical center hospitals, he became the first director of the program in hospital administration at the University of Michigan in 1955. While at Michigan, he directed an important study of the hospital and medical economics of the state. This study received national attention and led to his being offered the presidency of the Blue Cross Association in 1961. For the next 20 years, McNerney built the association into a strong national organization of Blue Cross plans. In 1977, the Blue Cross Association merged with the Blue Shield Association, with McNerney serving as president of the new corporation.

McNerney serves on the boards of nine national companies and is chairman of American Health Properties. His current appointments include the advisory panel on the assessment of medical technology for the Office of Technology Assessment, commissioner of the Physician Payment Review Commission and the Commission on the Future Structure of Veterans' Health Care, and numerous other national boards and commissions. He is the recipient of numerous awards, including the Award of Merit from the Healthcare Planning Forum and the Award of Honor and Justice Ford Kimbell Awards of the American Hospital Association. McNerney received an M.H.A. in hospital administration from the University of Minnesota in 1950.

David Mechanic (1936–)

David Mechanic is a prominent medical sociologist especially interested in medical economics. He currently serves as the René Dubos professor of behavioral sciences at Rutgers University; director of the Institute for Health, Health Care Policy, and Aging Research; and director of the Center for the Organization and Financing of Care for the Seriously Mentally Ill. He is also adjunct professor of psychiatry at the Robert Wood Johnson Medical School and director of the Rutgers-Princeton Program in Mental Health Services Research Training. Mechanic is the former dean of the faculty of arts and sciences at Rutgers and was on the faculty of Princeton University and the University of Wisconsin. He has also held several short-term visiting professorships in foreign universities.

Mechanic is the recipient of numerous fellowships and academic honors, including the first Carl Taube Award, Mental Health Section, from the American Public Health Association in 1990 and the Distinguished Service Award from the Melvyn H. Motolinsky Research Foundation in 1987. He is a member of numerous professional organizations, including the National Academy of Sciences, and is a member of the Commission on Behavioral and Social Sciences Education for the National Research Council and the Robert Wood Johnson Foundation Commission on Medical Education. He is listed in *Who's Who in America* and serves on several editorial boards. His current research interests include the organization of medical and psychiatric care, adaptation to stress, decision-making processes in medicine and psychiatry, illness behavior, and comparative medical organization.

Mechanic received a Ph.D. from Stanford University in 1959. He has written many books, including *From Advocacy to Allocation: The Evolving American Health Care System* (1986), *Painful Choices in Health Care: Research Essays on the Sociology of Health Care* (1989), *Paying for Services: Promises and Pitfalls of Capitation* (1989), plus numerous papers, reports, and journal articles.

Marcia G. Ory (1950–)

Marcia G. Ory is chief of the Social Science Research on Aging, Behavioral and Social Research Program at the National Institute on Aging, National Institutes of Health, in Bethesda, Maryland. She received a Ph.D. in behavioral sciences from Purdue University in 1976 and a master's in public health from Johns Hopkins University in 1981. Active in professional organizations, Ory also serves on several national task forces and advisory boards, including the Alzheimer's Disease and Related Disorders Association Health Services Research Task Force, the Surgeon General's Workshop on Health Promotion and Aging, and the World Health Organization project on health behavior research and indicators. Her major areas of interest and research are aging and health care, health and behavior research, and gender differences in health and longevity. She believes that additional research on new and evolving forms of health care for the growing population of older people is needed to inform important policy decisions in this field.

From 1981 to 1986, Ory served as program director for the Biosocial Aging and Health Section, Behavioral Sciences Research Program, at the National Institutes of Health. She was a professor of public health at the University of North Carolina and the University of Alabama. She has been active in numerous professional organizations and currently chairs the American Public Health Association. Her many honors include listings in *Who's Who of American Women, NIH Women in Science, American Men and Women of Science,* and *International Leaders in Achievement.* She has written numerous books and articles.

June E. Osborn (1937–)

June E. Osborn is dean and professor of epidemiology at the School of Public Health at the University of Michigan and professor of pediatrics and communicable diseases at the University of Michigan Medical School. She has also held faculty and administrative appointments at the University of Wisconsin. An expert on the AIDS epidemic, Osborn is a member of the Global Commission on AIDS for the World Health Organization and chair of the National Commission on AIDS. She recently served on the AIDS Research Advisory Committee for the National Institutes of Health and was a member of the National Advisory Committee for the AIDS Health Services Program for the Robert Wood Johnson Foundation, as well as serving on numerous other boards and committees.

Osborn received her M.D. from Case Western Reserve University School of Medicine in 1961. She is listed in *Who's Who in America* and has received many awards and lectureships. She has written numerous scientific papers and articles, many focusing on AIDS.

Mark V. Pauly (1941–)

One of the nation's leading health economists, Mark V. Pauly is professor and chairman of health care systems and professor of insurance and public management at the Wharton School and professor of economics in the School of Arts and Sciences at the University of Pennsylvania. He is also executive director of the Leonard Davis Institute of Health Economics and the Robert D.

Eilers professor of health care management and economics. He received his Ph.D. in economics from the University of Virginia in 1967. His expertise is in medical economics, insurance theory and regulation, public finance, and collective decision making.

Pauly has been elected a member of the Institute of Medicine of the National Academy of Sciences and serves on the editorial boards of *Public Finance Quarterly, Health Services Research, Journal of Health Economics,* and the *Journal of Risk and Uncertainty.* He is also a board member of the Association for Health Services Research and the Hospital Research Foundation, in addition to being a member of the Council on Research and Development of the American Hospital Association. He is the author of *Doctors and Their Workshops* (1980) and coauthor of *Controlling Medicaid Costs: Federalism, Competition and Choice* (1983) and *Lessons from the First Twenty Years of Medicare: Research Implications for Public and Private Sector Policy* (1988).

Edmund Pellegrino (1920–)

A noted ethicist, physician, and educator, Edmund Pellegrino is currently director of the Center for the Advanced Study of Ethics at Georgetown University and John Carroll professor of medicine and medical humanities at Georgetown University Medical Center. Prior to his appointment at Georgetown University, he was president of the Catholic University of America and president and chairman of the board of directors of Yale-New Haven Medical Center, as well as professor of medicine at Yale University School of Medicine. He also serves as chairman of the board of directors for the Institute on Human Values in Medicine and served as chairman of the National Academy of Sciences' Institute of Medicine Committee on Social Ethics in Health.

Pellegrino is the recipient of numerous awards, including the American Medical Association Award to Outstanding Contributors to Allied Health Education and Accreditation, the Mercy Hospital Foundation Medal of Excellence, and the Presidential Medal from Georgetown University. He is currently a member of over 30 committees and boards, serves on 19 editorial boards, and has been the recipient of numerous honorary degrees.

Pellegrino received his M.D. from New York University College of Medicine in 1944. He is listed in *Who's Who in America, American Men and Women in Science,* and other prestigious directories. He is the author of approximately 200 editorial contributions, articles, and reviews in scientific research, medical education, and philosophy. Recent book titles include *For the Patient's Good: The Restoration of Beneficence in Health Care* (1987) and *Catholic Perspectives on Medical Morals: Foundational Issues* (co-author, 1989).

Claude Denson Pepper (1901–1989)

Serving as Florida's U.S. senator from 1936 to 1950 and as a member of the House of Representatives from 1962 to 1989, Claude Denson Pepper took an active interest in health care throughout his long legislative career. He introduced the concept that was to become Medicare 36 years before it became law and continued throughout his career to champion the nation's older citizens. As chairman of the Senate Subcommittee on Wartime Health and Education, he was involved in the first recommendations for national health insurance, for home care as an essential component of the health care system, and for "capitation," or the use of a set fee in financing the health care system. His committee's recommendation that the government play a major role in financing research aimed at preventing and curing disease led to the expansion of the National Institutes of Health. Appearing on the cover of *Time* in 1938 and again in 1983, he was characterized as leaving "a legacy of help for the aged." At the time of his death, he was chairman of the Pepper Commission, which has proposed a new version of universal health insurance.

A major national political figure over a longer span of time than any modern figure in the United States, Pepper continued to propose sweeping solutions to the nation's health care crisis until his death at age 88. The year before he died, his long-term health care bill was defeated in the House, although his impassioned speech defending it received a standing ovation.

Paul Ramsey (1913–1988)

Paul Ramsey taught in the Department of Religion at Princeton University from 1944 until 1982 and was chairman of that department from 1959 to 1963. He was also a senior fellow of the Council of the Humanities from 1958 to 1959 and a McCosh Faculty Fellow from 1955 to 1966. As a teacher, he was known for his fundamental course in Christian ethics. As an author and lecturer, he was a leading voice in continuing discussions about medical ethics until his death in 1988 and was well-known for his stance against using new birth technologies. Ramsey was also active in helping to develop two institutions dedicated to contemporary ethical concerns, the Hastings Center and the Kennedy Center at Georgetown University, where he held an appointment in the medical school.

Ramsey obtained a Ph.D. from Yale University in 1943. His publications include *Fabricated Man: The Ethics of Genetic Control* (1970), *The Patient as Person: Explorations in Medical Ethics* (1970), *The Ethics of Fetal Research* (1975), and *The Ethics at the Edge of Life* (1977).

Uwe Reinhardt (1937–)

Uwe Reinhardt has been a professor of economics at Princeton University since 1968. A member of the National Leadership Commission on Health Care and of the Physician Payment Review Commission, he has focused much of his attention on health care issues. He has served on the editorial board for several health care journals, including *Health and Society, Health Affairs, Patient Care, Health Policy and Education,* and the *Journal of Health Economics.*

Reinhardt received a Ph.D. in economics from Yale University in 1970. From 1979 to 1981, he served on the Department of Health, Education, and Welfare's National Health Care Technology Council, and in 1981 he became a member of the Department of Health and Human Services' Private Sector Task Force on Health Policy. Reinhardt served on the governing council of the National Academy of Sciences from 1979 to 1982. He is listed in *Who's Who in America.* His publications include *Physician Productivity and the Demand for Health Manpower* (1975) plus numerous journal articles.

Arnold Relman (1923–)

The editor-in-chief of the *New England Journal of Medicine* since 1988, Arnold Relman has written widely on the economic, ethical, legal, and social aspects of health care. He has served on the faculty at Boston University, the University of Pennsylvania School of Medicine, and Harvard Medical School. He has served as director of the V and VI Medical Services at Boston City Hospital and as senior physician at the Brigham and Women's

Hospital in Boston. Relman is a fellow of the American Academy of Arts and Sciences, a member of the Institute of Medicine of the National Academy of Sciences, and a former president of the American Federation for Clinical Research, the American Society of Clinical Investigation, and the Association of American Physicians. He is on the board of directors of the Hastings Center for Bioethics and is a trustee of Columbia University and of the Boston University and University of Pennsylvania Medical Centers.

Relman received his M.D. degree from Columbia University in 1946 and holds honorary degrees from numerous institutions. He has received many awards, including the Distinguished Service Award of the American College of Cardiology in 1987, and he is listed in *Who's Who in America*. He is the editor of several publications and is a contributor to journals, including the *New England Journal of Medicine*.

Dorothy P. Rice (1922–)

Dorothy P. Rice is currently a professor in the Department of Social and Behavioral Sciences, with joint appointments at the Institute for Health and Aging and the Institute for Health Policy Studies at the University of California, San Francisco. She served as director of the National Center for Health Statistics from January 1976 to June 1982, where she led in the development and management of a nationwide health care information system. During her stewardship at the center, she was internationally recognized as the key architect of the National Health Expenditure Survey. She also developed the methodology for the government's Cost of Illness Survey. Before joining the National Center for Health Statistics, Rice served as deputy assistant commissioner for research and statistics at the Social Security Administration. She advocates a congressional restructuring of Medicare, maintaining that the medical care needs of the elderly are changing. When Medicare went into effect, it was essentially a health insurance plan for acute illness; today's elderly live longer, and chronic diseases afflict more of them.

A graduate of the University of Wisconsin in 1941, Rice has received numerous awards, including the American Public Health Association Sedgwick Memorial Medal and the Association for Health Services Research Presidential Award for Leadership and Contributions to Health Services Research. She is listed in *Who's Who in America* and other prestigious directories. Throughout her career of public service, she has served on numerous committees and advisory boards. She has testified before Congress on health care issues many times and serves on the editorial boards of four publications. She has written numerous reports, journal articles, professional papers, books, and monographs.

John D. (Jay) Rockefeller IV (1937–)

The senator and former governor of West Virginia has had a long career of public service. Jay Rockefeller served as a member of the national advisory council on the Peace Corps in 1961, on the Bureau for Far Eastern Affairs in 1963, and on several commissions related to youth in the late 1960s. Rockefeller was governor of his state from 1976 to 1984 and has served as senator since 1984. He has served on various committees, including the Finance Committee, for which he is chairman of the subcommittee on Medicare and long-term care, and as a member of the subcommittee on health for families and the uninsured. Rockefeller is currently chairman of the Bipartisan Commission on Comprehensive Health Care (Pepper Commission) and chairman of the National Commission on Children.

Rockefeller graduated from Harvard University in 1961 with a B.A. in Far Eastern languages and history. He holds numerous honorary degrees and is listed in *Who's Who in America*.

Carl J. Schramm

Carl J. Schramm is president of the Health Insurance Association of America, the trade group representing the nation's commercial health insurance companies. Prior to assuming his current post in 1987, he was the founder and director of the Johns Hopkins Center for Hospital Finance and Management and was associate professor of health policy and management at Johns Hopkins University. Schramm's experience in government began as a staff economist to the National Commission of State Workmen's Compensation Law. He has also worked for the Senate Committee on Labor and Human Resources and served nine years as a member and chairman of the Maryland Health Services Cost Review Commission. He was recently appointed to the U.S. Labor Department Commission, commonly known as the Coal Commission. He holds positions on several boards, including the

Wellness Councils of America, National Hospice Organization, Center for Corporate Public Involvement, Life and Health Insurance Medical Research Fund, Leonard Davis Institute at the Wharton School of Business, the University of Pennsylvania, and the National Library of Medicine.

Schramm received his Ph.D. in economics from the University of Wisconsin in 1973 and his J.D. from Georgetown Law School in 1978. He founded Health Care Investment Analysts, which is now a subsidiary of Citicorp. He authored *Health Care and Its Cost* (1987), coauthored *Workers Who Drink* (1978), and has written other books and journal articles on the subjects of health care financing, capital formation, alcoholism, public health policy, and health insurance.

Henry Simmons (1930–)

Henry Simmons is president of the National Leadership Commission on Health Care, which is a private bipartisan group seeking to address the problems of cost, quality, and access to health care in the United States. He is also visiting research professor at the School of Government and Business at George Washington University. Formerly vice-president and director of the Health Care Division at Sears World Trade, Inc., he has held several other major positions in both business and academe. From 1970 to 1975, he held various posts in the Department of Health, Education, and Welfare (HEW). Simmons is the recipient of numerous honors and awards, including the Food and Drug Administration and HEW Awards of Merit. He has served on numerous national committees, including the Committee to Plan a Private/Public Sector Entity for Technology Assessment in Medical Care and the Institute of Medicine of the National Academy of Sciences. He is on the editorial board of *Forum on Medicine* of the American College of Physicians. Simmons received an M.D. from the University of Pittsburgh in 1957 and an M.P.H. from Harvard in 1964.

Fredrick J. Stare (1910–)

The cofounder of the American Council on Science and Health, Fredrick J. Stare is a nutritionist, biochemist, and physician. He is currently professor of nutrition emeritus at Harvard's Department of Nutrition, which he founded. He has taught at a number of prestigious institutions in both the United States and Europe, including a 34-year stint as chairman of the Department of

Nutrition at Harvard Medical School from 1942 to 1976. Stare has served on a number of boards and commissions, including the Food and Nutrition Board of the National Research Council. He has served as consultant to numerous voluntary and governmental agencies, and to a number of food companies. Stare was cofounder and moderator of the syndicated radio program "Healthline." The recipient of numerous honors, he most recently won the Medal of Honor from the International Foundation for Nutrition Research and Education.

Stare received a Ph.D. from the University of Wisconsin in 1934 and an M.D. from the University of Chicago in 1941. He is listed in *Who's Who in America*. He has written numerous textbooks and a nationally syndicated column. Recent titles he has coauthored include *Eat OK—Feel OK! Food Facts and Your Health* (1978), *The 100% Natural, Purely Organic, Cholesterol-Free, Megavitamin, Low-Carbohydrate Nutrition Hoax* (1983), and *Balanced Nutrition: Beyond the Cholesterol Scare* (1989).

Bernard R. Tresnowski (1932–)

Bernard R. Tresnowski is president and chief executive officer of the Blue Cross and Blue Shield Association, the national coordinating organization for the nationwide network of Blue Cross and Blue Shield plans. He became president of the association in 1981, having joined the Blue Cross Association in 1967 as head of its Medicare division. Tresnowski became senior vice-president in 1969 and executive vice-president in 1977, when consolidation with the Blue Shield Association occurred. Prior to joining Blue Cross, Tresnowski served in administrative positions at the Albert Einstein Medical Center in Philadelphia and at the St. Joseph Mercy Hospital in Pontiac, Michigan. He received a master's degree in public health and hospital administration at the University of Pittsburgh in 1958.

Tresnowski is a member of the American College of Healthcare Executives and received the Silver Medal Award for excellence and leadership from that organization in 1990. He serves as president of the International Federation of Voluntary Health Service Funds, is a principal in the Dunlop Group of Six, and is a member of the National Advisory Panel of the Brookings Institution as well as numerous other health-related organizations. He has written numerous articles and chapters on health care issues in books and professional journals.

Robert M. Veatch (1939–)

Robert M. Veatch is director and professor of medical ethics at the Kennedy Institute and professor in the philosophy department and the medical school at Georgetown University. He received his Ph.D. from Harvard University in 1971 and has taught at Harvard and Columbia Universities. Veatch served as staff director of the Research Group on Death and Dying at the Hastings Center from 1970 to 1979. He has served on the editorial boards of *JAMA*, the *Journal of Medicine and Philosophy*, the *Harvard Theological Review*, the *Journal of Religious Ethics*, and other publications.

Veatch is a member of the board of directors for Hospice Care of Washington, a member of the Ethics Committee at the Department of Pediatrics at Georgetown Hospital, and a member of the District of Columbia Commission of Public Health Task Force on Organ/Tissue Donation and Transplantation as well as numerous other organizations. He has been listed in *Who's Who in America* and received the National Book Award from the American Medical Writers Association in 1978. His publications include *Case Studies in Medical Ethics* (1977), *A Theory of Medical Ethics* (1981), *Case Studies of Nursing Ethics* (1987), *Foundations of Justice* (1987), *The Patient as Partner* (1987), *Cross Cultural Perspectives in Medical Ethics* (editor, 1989), and *Death, Dying, and the Biological Revolution* (editor, 1989).

Henry Waxman (1939–)

Henry Waxman has been a U.S. congressman from California since 1974. He is chairman of the House Subcommittee on Health and the Environment, which deals with health and environmental issues, and is a member of the Select Committee on Aging. Waxman has been involved in health care issues since 1969, when he was named to the California State Assembly Health Committee, which he later chaired. In Congress, he has worked to improve Medicare and Medicaid programs, fighting attempts to reduce benefits and coverage of these programs. He has supported legislation for improved prenatal and infant care for low-income citizens, protection against impoverishment for the spouses of persons in nursing homes, more community services for people needing long-term care, and prescription drug coverage under Medicare for people with high drug expenditures. He is a leader of efforts to improve the quality of nursing homes and home health services.

Waxman received a bachelor's degree in political science from UCLA in 1961 and a J.D. from the UCLA Law School in 1964. He is listed in *Who's Who in America*. Prior to his election to Congress, he served three terms in the California State Assembly, where he was also active in supporting health care legislation.

Elizabeth M. Whelan (1943–)

Elizabeth M. Whelan is the president of the American Council on Science and Health and served as director of that organization from 1977 to 1989. The council is a national nonprofit educational organization promoting scientifically balanced evaluations of food, chemicals, the environment, and human health. Whelan received an Sc.D. degree from Harvard School of Public Health in 1971. She is listed in *Who's Who in America*.

Whelan serves as the moderator of "Healthline," a nationally syndicated radio program that airs on 100 stations, and is a member of several national committees, including the American Cancer Society's National Committee on Cancer Prevention and Detection. She is the recipient of the Early Career Award from the American Public Health Association, the Distinguished Achievement Award from Connecticut College, and the American Medical Writers Walter Alvarez Award for Excellence in Medical Communication. Her numerous media appearances include the "McNeil-Lehrer News Hour," "Today," "Good Morning America," and "60 Minutes." She has appeared on local television and radio talk programs across the nation. Her publications include *Panic in the Pantry: Food Facts, Fads and Fallacies* (coauthor, 1977), *Eat OK—Feel OK! Food Facts and Your Health* (coauthor, 1978), *Preventing Cancer: What You Can Do To Cut Your Risk by Up to 50%* (1978), *A Baby? . . . Maybe* (1980), *The 100% Natural, Purely Organic, Cholesterol-Free, Megavitamin, Low-Carbohydrate Nutrition Hoax* (coauthor, 1983), *A Smoking Gun* (1984), *Toxic Terror* (1986), and *Balanced Nutrition: Beyond the Cholesterol Scare* (coauthor, 1989).

Gail R. Wilensky (1943–)

Gail R. Wilensky is the administrator of the Health Care Financing Administration (HCFA). In that capacity, she directs the

Medicare and Medicaid programs and serves as a key health policy adviser to the secretary of health and human services and other top administration officials. She is a nationally recognized expert on a wide range of health policy issues and is listed in *Who's Who in America.*

Wilensky previously served as senior research manager at the Health and Human Services National Center for Health Services Research, where she designed and directed the analysis of the National Medical Care Expenditure Survey. She came to HCFA from Project HOPE, where she was vice-president for the division of health affairs. She has served on the faculties of the University of Michigan and George Washington University and held a senior research appointment at the Urban Institute. She is a member of the Institute of Medicine of the National Academy of Sciences and was a member of the Physician Payment Review Commission and the Health Advisory Committee of the General Accounting Office. She received a Ph.D. in economics at the University of Michigan in 1968. She has written many articles on health economics and health policy.

4

Facts and Data

THE FEDERAL GOVERNMENT COMPILES FACTS and data related to health care on an ongoing basis. In addition, states, local governments, and private organizations compile statistical information. Included in this chapter is a separate section containing tables (beginning on page 75) and figures (beginning on page 80) that reflect the magnitude of the health care crisis and its complexity. The factors contributing to the crisis are inextricably interrelated and constantly changing. Critics who single out one factor as the major cause of the crisis (e.g., physicians' fees, government regulation, insurance costs, malpractice litigation) are overlooking the interdependent nature of the myriad aspects of our pluralistic health care system.

Statistics

Rising costs are usually cited first when discussing the causes of the health care crisis. These costs can be quantified in several ways. Figure 1 relates costs to the Consumer Price Index (CPI) and the gross national product (GNP). Since 1982, medical care has consistently remained several percentage points higher than "all items" in the CPI. National health expenditures rose from $248.1 billion a year in 1980 to an estimated $662 billion in 1990. That amounts to approximately $2,354 per person.

Table 1 shows that by 1988, national health expenditures were 11.1 percent of the GNP. According to the Health Care Financing Administration, that figure rose to an estimated 12 percent by 1990 and continues to increase. Table 1 also shows a breakdown of the rise in specific categories of health expenditures. Nursing home care, for example, cost $1 billion in 1960 and had risen to $43.1 billion by 1988. Program administration and the net cost of private health insurance rose from $1.2 billion in 1960 to $26.3 billion in 1988.

Figure 2 breaks out the costs of hospital expenditures and physician services from 1980 to 1990. Including both inpatient and outpatient costs, hospital expenditures rose from $101.6 billion in 1980 to $252 billion in 1990. Physician services experienced a similar rise, with services soaring from $46.8 billion in 1980 to $148 billion in 1990.

Since large numbers are hard to assimilate, it is helpful to discuss health care costs on a per-person basis. In 1980, for example, the expense per person was $1,059. In 1985 it was $1,700 per person. By 1989 it had risen to $2,354 per person—the highest figure of any developed nation. (Figures from 1989 are the most recent figures available from the Health Care Financing Administration.)

Again, to put statistics into a form understandable to the average reader, Table 2 is included to show the cost per patient for specific treatments in 1989. One patient could expect to spend $40,000 for hip fracture treatment and rehabilitation, or $30,000 for coronary bypass surgery.

These rising costs show no signs of abating. As seen in Table 3, the federal government is predicting that national health expenditures will rise from $647.3 billion in 1990 to $1,529.3 billion in the year 2000. Such increases are a symptom of malaise that cannot be cured by cost containment alone. In the 1980s, the government attempted to cut costs by curtailing Medicare and Medicaid programs, introducing the diagnosis-related group (DRG) concept in hospitalization, and encouraging competition in the health care marketplace. Costs continued to rise. Many experts in the health care field deplore the government's tendency to approach the health care crisis with cost-containment measures. What is needed is a national health care policy to provide an overview of where the country is heading.

Changes in the health care system complicate attempts to gain an overview of the crisis. Almost as soon as a new factor is taken into account, it changes again. For example, in the early 1980s, health maintenance organizations (HMOs) were seen by many as a partial solution to the health care crisis. HMOs boomed by the end of the decade but did not take over the market as some had predicted. In fact, as shown in Figure 3, the number of operating HMOs fell 5.5 percent from 1988 to 1989, demonstrating a continued consolidation in the industry. The number of operating HMOs had fallen 6.8 percent in 1988 after increasing 12 percent in 1987 and 29 percent in 1986. Fewer HMOs were under development at the end of 1989 than at any time since the mid-1970s, when passage of federal legislation spurred the growth of the industry.

Insurance is another sector of the health care field that is changing rapidly. The share of personal health care paid by private health insurance as measured in the national health accounts continued to grow throughout the 1980s. In an effort to control costs, employers increased premium cost sharing to save money and to encourage employee awareness of the rising costs of health benefits. As shown in Table 4, employees found their deductible costs continuing to rise. Increasingly, many others found themselves without insurance at all. By 1989, experts estimated that 37 million Americans had no medical insurance, and 13.5 million of them went without crucial care because they could not afford it.

The roles of the significant players in the health care field are changing as well. The majority of physicians no longer belong to the American Medical Association, while specialty societies are growing in strength. As shown in Table 5, the fields doctors will choose to specialize in are predicted to change significantly. And the formerly male bastion of medicine is disappearing, with the percentage of female physicians predicted to increase 91.9 percent by the end of the century. For many physicians, the growth of HMOs and preferred provider organizations (PPOs) and the increased government regulation aimed at curtailing costs are decreasing their income, status, and autonomy. The threat of malpractice suits, increasing insurance costs, and heightened competition as a surplus of physicians emerges are all changing the physician's role as the former kingpin of the health care system.

Unlike their physician counterparts, nurses are in short supply. The current nursing shortage was recognized in 1986, when the vacancy rate for budgeted registered nurse (RN) positions in hospitals reached 11 percent. That figure was nearly triple the 3.7 percent vacancy rate in 1983. The U.S. Department of Health and Human Services estimates that hospitals need some 116,600 additional full-time RNs, while nursing homes require an additional 20,800. In mid-1987, a survey by the American Hospital Association (AHA) found that 54.3 percent of hospitals encountered a moderate or severe nursing shortage, experiencing vacancy rates of 10 percent or greater. The shortage is more pronounced in public hospitals. It was responsible for temporary bed closures in more than 18 percent of the nation's large urban hospitals, compared with 9.5 percent of the rural hospitals surveyed by the AHA in 1987. Emergency departments were temporarily closed in 14 percent of the hospitals in major urban areas. Federal estimates say that the supply of RNs with bachelor's degrees will fall 257,000 short of the demand by the year 2000.

In addition to rising costs and changing roles of health care providers, another major factor is having a great impact on the health care crisis. The growing numbers of elderly and their needs for long-term care will add increasing demands to an already overburdened system. The U.S. Bureau of the Census projects that the percentage of the population over age 65 will increase from 11.2 percent in 1980 to 18.3 percent in the year 2030. (See Table 6.) The burden this will place on the health care system is already apparent in currently available data. As shown in Table 7, the percentage of people aged 85 or over enrolled in Medicare continues to rise.

Obviously, the elderly population will experience more chronic conditions than younger people, but another factor surfaces as well. As shown in Figure 4, lower-income people tend to have a higher rate of chronic conditions. Quality of care and unequal access are both unfortunate components of the current health care crisis. The Robert Wood Johnson Foundation issued a special report, *Access to Health Care in the United States: Results of a 1986 Survey,* which found that although Americans are generally satisfied with the care they receive, the poor, minorities, and the uninsured are experiencing a decline in access to health care. Those who traditionally have had trouble obtaining care are facing significant financial burdens in paying for the care they do secure. (See Table 8.) The report cites several trends that are eroding aspects of the system that previously enabled many providers to care for many poor patients. These trends include:

1. Age. Children under 17 are more likely to have a regular source of care than other age groups. Those least likely

to have a regular source of care range from 17 to 64. Although half the elderly reported having a chronic or serious illness, their average number of ambulatory visits is the same as adults under 65.

2. Residence. Urban and rural Americans have approximately equal access to the health care system; however, a larger portion of rural people are in poor health.

3. Gender. Men are without a regular source of health care at a significantly higher rate than women. Men also make fewer ambulatory visits than women.

4. Ethnicity. The situation for Hispanics is worsening, with the percentage of those without a regular source of care almost double that for non-Hispanic whites. Blacks are substantially worse off than non-Hispanic whites and have fewer ambulatory visits than other groups, despite high rates of chronic illness.

5. Insurance. Uninsured Americans are almost twice as likely to be without a regular source of care than the insured. They also have 27 percent fewer ambulatory visits and a slightly higher rate of medical emergencies.

6. Chronic or Serious Illness. Nearly 16 percent of people with a chronic or serious illness did not have an ambulatory visit in the year prior to being interviewed.

The rising incidence of AIDS and the accompanying cost of treatment will have a major effect on the health care crisis. Predictions of the extent of infection vary, but dealing with this new epidemic will undoubtedly contribute to the health care crisis.

Surveys and Commission Reports

Numerous surveys have been taken and commissions established to gather information about various factors contributing to the health care crisis. Two of particular importance are listed in this chapter: (1) the 1983 report of the President's Commission on the Ethical and Legal Problems in Medicine and Biomedical and Behavioral Research and (2) the report of the National Leadership Commission on Health Care.

Extensive in scope and well-written, the President's Commission on Ethical and Legal Problems in Medicine and Biomedical and Behavioral Research is referred to constantly in health care literature. The study, which was undertaken from 1980 to 1983, is published in 11 volumes and includes 9 reports. The health care section includes a definition of death, informed consent, genetic screening counseling, differences in availability of health care, life-sustaining treatment, privacy, and confidentiality. The biomedical and behavioral research section includes genetic engineering, compensation for injured subjects, and whistle-blowing in research.

Three basic principles predominate the report:

1. That the well-being of people be promoted
2. That people's value preferences and choices be respected
3. That people be treated equitably

In brief, the commission concluded:

- Society has an ethical obligation to ensure equitable access to health care for all

- The societal obligation is balanced by individual obligations

- Equitable access to health care requires that all citizens be able to secure an adequate level of care without excessive burdens

- When equity occurs through the operation of private forces, there is no need for government involvement, but the ultimate responsibility for ensuring that society's obligation is met, through a combination of public- and private-sector arrangements, rests with the federal government

- The cost of achieving equitable access to health care ought to be shared fairly

- Efforts to contain rising health care costs are important, but should not focus on limiting the attainment of equitable access for the least well-served portion of the public

The report of the National Leadership Commission on Health Care, 1986–1989, was published in book form as *For the Health of a Nation: A Shared Responsibility* (listed in Chapter 6 of this book). In 1986, a group of concerned citizens formed a commission to propose workable solutions to major problems in health care. Members were drawn from both the private and public sectors and included representatives from health care, business, law, economics, politics, ethics, and labor. They identified three major problems in health care: cost, quality, and access to care. The commission's vision of health care for the twenty-first century included:

- A healthy society in a healthy environment

- Universal access to a basic level of care, providing a range of necessary services, including preventive, acute, chronic, and mental health care

- Vigorous public education, emphasizing preventive care, healthy life-styles, and appropriate levels of care

- Appropriate care based on general agreement, resulting from solid scientific assessments of what procedures and technologies are considered effective

- An innovative, efficient health care system that operates in a culture of continuous improvement

- Resolution of the malpractice crisis so that malpractice concerns are no longer a consideration in health care delivery

- Patient contributions to the cost of their care, although only a minimal amount for the poorest, so that patients feel individual responsibility for their care

- Affordable health care

- Controlled costs, emphasizing payment for appropriate, efficient care

- A high level of personal responsibility for health care and for understanding the options, costs, and benefits of health care decisions

- A strong doctor-patient relationship based on trust and a well-informed patient

- A strong public-private partnership dedicated to expanding access, controlling costs, and improving the quality of health care

To date, both of these reports have received widespread acclaim, but no national policy has emerged to implement their goals. Many ethical questions remain unanswered, and unequal access to quality care continues to be a major problem in the United States today.

Other Resources

The National Center for Health Statistics publishes data about health care in numerous forms. Many reports can be found in the *Vital and Health Statistics* series, which includes over 500 individual publications grouped into several subseries. Also available are *Advance Data from Vital and Health Statistics* and *Monthly Vital Statistics Report*. A free catalog is also available. Many of the reports can be found in libraries and selected institutions. For information about the availability of data from the center, contact:

Scientific and Technical Information Branch
Division of Data Services
National Center for Health Statistics
6526 Belcrest Road
Hyattsville, MD 20782
(301) 436-8500

Other excellent government sources of facts and data about health care are the *Statistical Abstract of the U.S.* (annual), the *American Statistics Index* (annual), and publications of the Office of Technology Assessment (OTA). Both statistical volumes are listed in Chapter 6, while the OTA is listed in Chapter 5 of this book.

The American Hospital Association and the American Medical Association are excellent private sources of information (see Chapter 5). See also the *Statistical Bulletin*, which is published four times annually by the Metropolitan Life Insurance Company. Write to:

Statistical Bulletin
428 East Preston Street
Baltimore, MD 21202

TABLES

TABLE 1   National Health Expenditures, by Type of Expenditure, Selected Calendar Years 1960–1988, Billions of Dollars

Spending category	1960	1970	1980	1985	1986	1987	1988
National health expenditures	$27.1	$74.4	$249.1	$420.1	$450.5	$488.8	$539.9
Health services/ supplies	25.4	69.1	237.8	404.7	434.5	471.6	520.5
Personal health care	23.9	64.9	218.3	367.2	397.7	434.7	478.3
Hospital care	9.3	27.9	102.4	167.9	179.3	193.7	211.8
Physician services	5.3	13.6	41.9	74.0	82.1	93.0	105.1
Dentist services	2.0	4.7	14.4	23.3	24.7	27.1	29.4
Other professional services	0.6	1.5	8.7	16.6	18.3	20.2	22.5
Home health care	0.0	0.1	1.3	3.8	4.0	4.2	4.4
Drugs and other nondurable medical products	4.2	8.8	20.1	32.3	35.6	38.6	41.9
Vision products/other medical durables	0.8	2.0	5.0	8.4	9.5	9.8	10.8
Nursing home care	1.0	4.9	20.0	34.1	36.7	39.7	43.1
Other personal health care	0.7	1.4	4.6	6.8	7.6	8.4	9.3
Program administration and net cost of private health insurance	1.2	2.8	12.2	25.2	23.4	22.4	26.3
Gov't public health	0.4	1.4	7.2	12.3	13.5	14.5	15.9
Research and construction	1.7	5.3	11.3	15.4	16.0	17.2	19.4
National health expenditures as a percentage of GNP	5.3%	7.3%	9.1%	10.5%	10.6%	10.8%	11.1%
National health expenditures per capita (dollars)*	$143	$346	$1,059	$1,700	$1,806	$1,941	$2,124

* Per capita figures are derived using July 1 Social Security area population estimates.

SOURCE: Health Care Financing Administration, Office of the Actuary.

TABLE 2   Costs of Treatment for Selected Preventable Conditions
            in 1989

Condition	Overall magnitude	Avoidable intervention*	Cost per patient**
Heart disease	7 million with coronary artery desiase 500,000 deaths/yr. 284,000 bypass procedures/yr.	Coronary bypass surgery	$30,000
Cancer	1 million new cases/yr. 510,000 deaths/yr.	Lung cancer treatment Cervical cancer treatment	$29,000 $28,000
Stroke	600,000 strokes/yr. 150,000 deaths/yr.	Hemiplegia treatment and rehabilitation	$22,000
Injuries	2.3 million hospitalizations/yr. 142,500 deaths/yr.	Quadriplegia treatment and rehabilitation (lifetime)	$570,000
	177,000 persons with spinal cord injuries in the United States	Hip fracture treatment and rehabilitation Severe head injury treatment and rehabilitation	$40,000 310,000
HIV infection	1–1.5 million infected 118,000 AIDS cases (as of Jan. 1990)	AIDS treatment (lifetime)	$75,000
Alcoholism	18.5 million abuse alcohol 105,000 alcohol-related deaths/yr.	Liver transplant	$250,000
Drug abuse	Regular users: 1–3 million, cocaine 900,000, IV drugs 500,000, heroin Drug-exposed babies: 375,000	Treatment of cocaine-exposed baby (5 years)	$66,000
Low-birth-weight baby	260,000 born/yr. 23,000 deaths/yr.	Neonatal intensive care	$10,000
Inadequate immunization	Lacking basic immunization series: 20%–30%, aged 2 and younger 3%, aged 6 and older	Congenital rubella syndrome treatment	$354,000 (lifetime)

* **Examples (other interventions may apply).**

** **Representative first-year costs, except as noted. Not indicated are nonmedical costs, such as lost productivity to society.**

SOURCE: Office of Disease Prevention and Health Promotion.

TABLE 3   Health Expenditures in the United States

Year	National health expenditures*	Federal health expenditures*	Federal share of total health expenditures
1965	$41.9	$5.5	13.1%
1970	75.0	17.7	23.6
1975	132.7	37.0	28.0
1980	248.1	71.0	28.6
1985	422.6	124.5	29.5
1990	647.3	195.5	30.2
1995	999.1	317.7	31.8
2000	1,529.3	498.6	32.6

* **Amounts in billions of dollars.**

SOURCE: National Health Expenditures, 1986–2000. *Health Care Financing Review,* Summer 1987.

TABLE 4   Percent of Full-Time Employees with Employer-Sponsored Health Insurance Coverage, by Amount of Deductible for Health Care Benefits, 1980–1988

Type and amount of deductible	1980	1982	1984	1988
Total	100%	100%	100%	100%
With annual deductible	100	100	99	94
$100 or less	85	85	72	51
Greater than $100	8	7	22	40
$101–$200	NA	NA	NA	31
Greater than $200	NA	NA	NA	9
Based on earnings	5	6	5	3
Without annual deductible	*	0	1	6
Deductible not on an annual basis	*	*	*	1
No deductible	*	0	1	5

* **Comparable data not available from published source.**

SOURCE: U.S. Department of Labor, Bureau of Labor Statistics, *Employee Benefits in Medium and Large Firms,* annual bulletins for 1980 and 1988 (Washington, DC: U.S. Government Printing Office).

TABLE 5   Projected Physician Population by Specialty, Sex
(Best Projection)

	1986	1990	2000	2010	1986–2000 % change
Total population	519,411	560,800	633,200	676,700	21.9%
General/family practice	68,437	70,900	74,600	77,800	9.0
General internal medicine	71,879	78,900	92,500	102,100	28.7
Medical subspecialties	49,249	56,100	69,600	79,100	41.4
General surgery	32,859	34,000	34,900	34,700	6.2
Surgical subspecialties	66,643	71,200	77,200	78,800	15.8
Pediatrics	38,631	43,100	52,500	59,100	35.8
Obstetrics/gynecology	31,882	34,400	39,100	42,100	22.7
Radiology	24,073	26,500	30,600	32,900	27.3
Psychiatry	37,440	39,400	42,100	42,800	12.4
Anesthesiology	23,795	26,800	32,200	35,700	35.4
Pathology	16,387	17,100	17,900	17,600	9.1
Emergency medicine	12,343	14,600	19,200	22,500	55.2
Male	439,805	460,600	480,400	477,800	9.2
Female	79,606	100,300	152,700	198,900	91.9

SOURCE: W. D. Marder, P. R. Kletke, A. B. Silberger, R. J. Wilke, *Physician Supply and Utilization by Specialty: Trends and Projections*. (Chicago: American Medical Association, February 1988).

TABLE 6   The Age Factor: Forecast of the Over-65 Population
(1950–2030)

Year	Population over Age 65	Percentage of U.S. Population
1950	12,397,000	8.1%
1970	20,087,000	9.9
1980	24,927,000	11.2
2000	31,822,000	12.2
2010	34,837,000	12.7
2020	45,102,000	15.5
2030	55,024,000	18.3

SOURCE: U.S. Bureau of the Census.

TABLE 7   The Age Factor: Numbers and Percent Distribution of
Medicare Enrollees* for Selected Years 1966–1987

Year	Number of enrollees	Median age all enrollees	Total	65–69	70–74	75–79	80–84	85 or over
					Percent distribution by age			
1966	19,108,822	72.8	100	34.2	28.7	19.7	11.2	6.2
1973	21,814,825	73.1	100	33.5	26.5	19.8	12.4	7.8
1980	25,515,070	73.2	100	33.1	26.4	18.9	12.2	9.4
1986	28,791,162	73.5	100	31.8	26.2	19.4	12.4	10.2
1987	29,380,480	73.5	100	31.8	26.0	19.4	12.5	10.3
Percent average annual increase	2.1	—	—	1.7	1.6	2.0	2.6	4.6

* Includes enrollees with hospital insurance (Part A) only or both hospital insurance and supplementary medical insurance (Part B).

SOURCE: Health Care Financing Administration, Bureau of Data Management and Strategy: Data from the Office of Statistics and Data Management.

TABLE 8   Americans Having Trouble with the Health Care System

People who reported needing care but having difficulty obtaining it — 16.1%

People with economic barriers to receiving various kinds of health services — 7.8%

People who tried to get care, but could not, for financial reasons — .4%

People whose most recent health care encounter cost more than $1,500 in out-of-pocket expenses — .8%

People with chronic or serious illnesses who had no physician visit in the prior 12 months — 18.5%

Pregnant women who did not receive care during the first trimester of pregnancy — 15.8%

Children under 17 whose parents did not know if immunizations were up-to-date — 7.5%

SOURCE: Robert Wood Johnson Foundation, *Access to Health Care in the United States: Results of a 1986 Survey.*

FIGURES

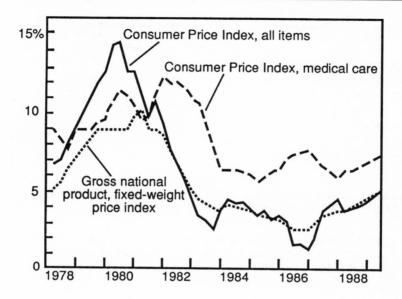

FIGURE 1   Changes in Measures of Price Inflation from the
Same Period of the Previous Year. *Sources:* U.S.
Departments of Labor and Commerce.

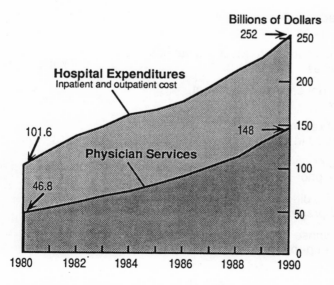

FIGURE 2   United States Medical Costs, 1980–1990. *Source:* U.S.
Department of Labor.

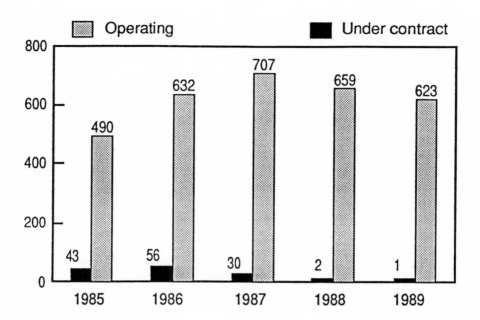

FIGURE 3   HMOs in the United States. *Source:* SMG Marketing
Group, Inc. © 1990.

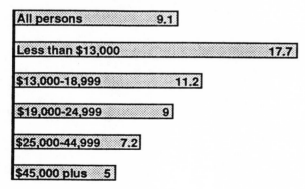

FIGURE 4   Percentage of People Who Experience Limitation of
Major Activity Due to a Chronic Condition, by Income
Level. *Source: Health, United States,* 1989.

5

Organizations, Associations, and Government Agencies

THIS IS A SELECTED LIST of nationally significant organizations, associations, and private and government agencies that are concerned with the health care crisis. Services and activities conducted by those listed include research, information services, public outreach, and the compilation of statistics. Some take a broad overview of the health care field, while others see the crisis from a particular perspective such as aging, ethics, business, or insurance. Although the groups below are representative of a broad spectrum of the health care field, it would be impossible to list every organization concerned with the health care crisis.

American Association of Healthcare Consultants (AAHC)
11208 Waples Mill Road, Suite 109
Fairfax, VA 22030
(703) 691-2247

AAHC is a national professional association representing over 200 individuals in more than 65 consulting firms working in the health care industry. Founded in 1949, it provides educational programs, services, and accreditation for members. Members are drawn from such specialties as strategic planning and marketing, organization and management, human resources management, facilities programming and planning, finance, and operations and information systems.

PUBLICATIONS: Annual directory of members and affiliated firms.

American Association of Preferred Provider Organizations (AAPPO)

111 East Wacker Drive, Suite 600
Chicago, IL 60601
(312) 644-6610

Founded in 1983, this national trade organization has well over 800 members that include preferred provider organizations (PPOs), insurance companies, doctors, hospitals, consultants, and pharmaceutical companies. It provides direction and assistance to the managed-care industry through education, information, research, and advocacy. It monitors state legislative activities and makes that information available to regional Preferred Provider associations.

PUBLICATIONS: *PPO Perspectives,* a bimonthly newsletter, plus numerous other publications, including *The Journal of the AAPPO, The PPO Primer!,* and a *Directory of Operational PPOs.* Also available to members are an annual summary of PPO legislation and the results of regular surveys.

American Association of Retired Persons (AARP)

601 E Street, NW
Washington, DC 20049
(202) 434-2277

This nonprofit, nonpartisan organization is dedicated to helping older Americans achieve lives of independence, dignity, and purpose. Founded in 1958, AARP is the nation's oldest and largest organization of older Americans, with a membership of more than 32 million. Health care is among the four major areas AARP has pinpointed as affecting the quality of life for older Americans. AARP is active in legislative advocacy and provides numerous services to members, such as a pharmacy service, group health insurance, and volunteer programs.

PUBLICATIONS: *Modern Maturity, AARP News Bulletin,* plus an annual catalog of books, booklets, and audiovisual materials, many of which cover health care issues.

American College of Physicians (ACP)

Independence Mall West
Sixth Street at Race
Philadelphia, PA 19106-1572
(800) 523-1546

The nation's largest medical specialty society works to uphold health care standards through activities in continuing education, health policy analysis, quality assurance, and medical technology assessment. Its 68,000 members include primary-care physicians and specialists in the various branches of internal medicine. ACP maintains a lobbying arm in Washington, D.C.

PUBLICATIONS: *Annals of Internal Medicine,* a monthly journal; *ACP Observer,* a monthly newspaper; and the *American College of Physicians Ethics Manual.*

American College of Preventive Medicine (ACPM)
1015 Fifteenth Street, NW, Suite 403
Washington, DC 20005
(202) 789-0003

This national professional society is for physicians committed to disease prevention and health promotion. It provides educational opportunities for members, advocates public policies consistent with the scientific principles of the discipline, and sponsors an annual preventive medicine review course.

PUBLICATIONS: *American Journal of Preventive Medicine,* a bimonthly journal, and the *Preventive Medicine Newsletter,* a quarterly review of legislation affecting preventive medicine and other news pertinent to members.

American Council on Science and Health (ACSH)
1995 Broadway, 16th Floor
New York, NY 10023-5860
(212) 362-7044

This consumer education organization is concerned with issues related to food, nutrition, chemicals, pharmaceuticals, life-style, the environment, and health. The independent, nonprofit organization consists of a board of 200 physicians, scientists, and policy advisers. These experts in a wide variety of fields review the council's reports and participate in ACSH seminars, press conferences, media communications, and other educational activities. Founded in 1978, the group grew out of a concern by scientists that important public policies related to health and the environment did not have a sound scientific basis. ACSH's research findings receive extensive coverage in the news media.

PUBLICATIONS: *Priorities* magazine plus a wide variety of publications and special reports whose topics range from AIDS to coronary heart disease to a survey of nutritional accuracy in U.S. magazines.

American Federation of Home Health Agencies (AFHHA)
1320 Fenwick Lane, Suite 500
Silver Spring, MD 20910
(301) 588-1454

Organized in 1981, AFHHA is a national organization representing Medicare-certified home health agencies in the legislative and regulatory process. It assists members with technical advice via a toll-free hot-line telephone number.

PUBLICATIONS: *Insider* and *Legislative Alert* newsletters.

American Health Care Association (AHCA)
1201 L Street, NW
Washington, DC 20005-4014
(202) 842-8444

Founded in 1949, AHCA is a federation of 51 affiliated associations representing 10,000 nonprofit and for-profit long-term-care providers. The nonprofit organization promotes standards for professionals and quality care for residents. AHCA is the largest publisher of career training and educational materials relating to long-term care.

PUBLICATIONS: *Provider Magazine* and *AHCA Notes,* plus numerous career training and educational materials.

American Health Foundation (AHF)
1 Dana Road
Valhalla, NY 10595
(914) 592-2600

Founded in 1969, AHF is a nonprofit research organization dedicated to preventive medicine. It comprises over 100 scientists from the fields of epidemiology, health education, biology, chemistry, and nutrition. The foundation focuses on identifying the causes of cancer, heart disease, and other major illnesses, and then developing strategies to reduce or eliminate the risk of these diseases. AHF scientists have concluded that what people eat and drink, whether they smoke, and how they conduct their daily lives relate to the incidence of avoidable chronic disease.

PUBLICATIONS: *Health Letter* and numerous brochures on reducing cholesterol and other ways to lead a longer, healthier life.

American Hospital Association (AHA)
840 North Lake Shore Drive
Chicago, IL 60611
(312) 280-6000

AHA's nearly 6,000 institutional members include hospitals, hospital-related long-term-care facilities, the corporate headquarters of health care systems, and hospital-related health care organizations. There are also 45,000 individual AHA members. Personal group members fall into specific categories such as societies for environmental services, food service administration, marketing, and public relations. AHA lobbies on behalf of hospitals and serves as a national voice for hospitals, answering over 250 media inquiries a month.

PUBLICATIONS: The *Complete AHA Catalog,* which features up to 60 pages of publications on a variety of topics; *AHA News;* and *Hospital.*

American Managed Care and Review Association (AMCRA)
1227 Twenty-fifth Street, NW, Suite 610
Washington, DC 20037
(202) 728-0506

As the national trade association for the managed-care industry, AMCRA represents more than 400 managed health care organizations. They include such organizations as health maintenance organizations (HMOs), preferred provider organizations (PPOs), utilization review companies, and organizations that provide services to the managed-care industry. AMCRA conducts educational conferences and actively represents the managed-care industry in legislative and regulatory issues. A special utilization review section of AMCRA monitors the utilization review industry and is contributing to the development of minimum standards and credentials for that segment of the managed-care industry.

PUBLICATIONS: *AMCRA Newsletter, HMO Trends Report, HMO Directory,* and *PPO Directory.*

American Medical Association (AMA)
515 North State Street
Chicago, IL 60610
(312) 645-4818

With a membership of 297,000, the AMA is the oldest organization for physicians in the nation. The group is extremely active in legislative advocacy and provides numerous information services and publications to keep members current. The AMA promotes medical education and seeks to enhance medical practices by offering workshops and other career resources to members. It also conducts surveys and makes results available to the public.

PUBLICATIONS: "Health Access America," published in 1990, is the AMA's proposal to improve access to affordable quality health care.

Other publications include *AMA Policy Compendium, Reference Guide to Policy and Official Statements, Physician and Public Attitudes on Health Care Issues, Current Opinions* by the AMA's Council on Ethical and Judicial Affairs, *American Medical News,* and the *Journal of the American Medical Association (JAMA).* The AMA also publishes a catalog of publications, products, and services.

American Nurses Association (ANA)
2420 Pershing Road
Kansas City, MO 64108
(816) 474-5720

This professional nurses' association works in various ways to address the interests of the nursing profession. ANA works to influence the development of national health policy, legislation, and regulations that will enable more people to have access to nursing care and ensure the quality of the health care services available. The organization works to set high standards of nursing practice, education, and service and disseminates a wide variety of information about nursing to the public. Founded in 1896, ANA has evolved into a registered labor organization. However, it does not directly represent nurses for collective bargaining purposes. It provides consultation and field services in labor relations.

PUBLICATIONS: A major player within health care publishing, ANA offers more than 150 books and audiovisual materials, which are listed in an annual catalog. Ten times a year, ANA publishes *The American Nurse,* its official newspaper, and *Capital Update,* a legislative newsletter.

American Pharmaceutical Association (APhA)
2215 Constitution Avenue, NW
Washington, DC 20037
(202) 628-4410

This professional society includes pharmacists, drug importers, educators, students, researchers, editors and publishers of pharmaceutical literature, pharmaceutical chemists and scientists, food and drug officials, hospital pharmacists, and pharmacists in governmental service. Founded in 1852, the 40,000-member organization promotes quality health care and rational drug therapy through the appropriate use of pharmacy services. APhA works to assure the quality of drug products, represents the interests of the industry in Congress, and disseminates information on developments in health care. It fosters professional education and training of pharmacists and supports three academies: the Academy of Pharmaceutical Research and Science, the Academy of Pharmacy Practice and Management, and the Academy of Students in Pharmacy.

PUBLICATIONS: *Academy Reporter,* a quarterly newsletter; *American Pharmacy,* a monthly journal; and numerous handbooks and reference books related to the pharmaceutical industry.

American Public Health Association (APHA)
1015 Fifteenth Street, NW
Washington, DC 20005
(202) 789-5600

Founded in 1872, APHA is the oldest and largest organization of public health professionals in the world, representing more than 32,000 members. Members include researchers, health service providers, administrators, teachers, and other health workers. APHA is concerned with a broad set of issues affecting personal and environmental health. In recent years, this has included such topics as state and federal funding for health programs, movement toward a national health program, air pollution control, promotion of water fluoridation, health care in jails and prisons, policies related to AIDS, and full funding for the World Health Organization. The organization reviews the scientific basis for public health programs and policies, identifies impending public health problems, and proposes solutions to technical problems.

PUBLICATIONS: APHA publishes an annual catalog with extensive listings of publications in the field of public health. It also publishes a monthly newsletter, *The Nation's Health.*

American Society on Aging (ASA)
833 Market Street, Suite 512
San Francisco, CA 94103
(415) 882-2910

ASA promotes the well-being of aging individuals and their families. The membership of over 8,000 includes public- and private-sector administrators and executives, service providers and researchers, educators and advocates, health and social service professionals, students, and the retired. ASA sponsors over 20 conferences and seminars annually on current developments in research, practice, policy, and theory. In addition to offering training, ASA gives its members access to special forums on religion and aging and business and aging. Several times a year, ASA sponsors several special projects to facilitate innovative approaches to serving the elderly.

PUBLICATIONS: *Generations* and *The Aging Connection.*

The Brookings Institution
1775 Massachusetts Avenue, NW
Washington, DC 20036-2188
(202) 797-6000

Three organizations merged in 1927 to form the Brookings Institution, a think tank concerned with public policy issues at a national level. Research programs involve some 50 full-time scholars and a staff of about 200, who work to identify problems before they become full-blown crises. They strive to impartially assess past policy successes and failures and anticipate consequences of alternative proposals. Fields of interest include economics, foreign policy, and governmental studies.

PUBLICATIONS: A complete list of *Brookings Books in Print* is available through the marketing department at (202) 797-6258. Although the publications cover a broad range, numerous titles are related to the health care crisis.

The Center for Medical Consumers
237 Thompson Street
New York, NY 10012
(212) 674-7105

The Center for Medical Consumers provides the public with an alternative source of medical and health information. Founded in 1976, this nonprofit organization came into being to help consumers cope with the rapid changes in technology and knowledge that make it difficult for doctors to keep current. Believing that medicine is as much art as science, the center promotes the idea that unquestioned acceptance of medical advice can place consumers at risk. It provides a medical library for consumers and a phone center that refers callers to other sources of information. The center does not make direct referrals to physicians or other practitioners, nor does it provide legal, financial, or medical advice.

PUBLICATIONS: *HealthFacts,* a monthly consumer newsletter, and special reports on timely issues.

Committee for National Health Insurance (CNHI)
1757 N Street, NW
Washington, DC 20036
(202) 223-9685

Formed in 1968, CNHI is committed to the revitalization of health care in the nation through reform of the organization and financing of health services under a cost-contained national health program. The committee conducts broad educational programs on problems and opportunities in the field of health care. Members constitute a cross section of the United States, representing labor (the original organizer of CNHI), business, women, youth, senior citizens, and educational, religious, and farm organizations. The organization has drafted a specific universal national health plan, the Health Security Partnership, which was proposed in April 1989.

PUBLICATIONS: Brochures about the Health Security Partnership and *Health Security News,* a bimonthly newsletter.

Concern for Dying (CFD)
250 West 57th Street
New York, NY 10107
(212) 246-6962

Founded in 1967, this organization of 250,000 members seeks to promote education toward "the prevention of the futile prolongation of the dying process and the assurance of patient autonomy in regard to treatment during terminal illness." It distributes the living will and educational literature and sponsors interdisciplinary programs for law, medical, nursing, social work, chaplaincy, and health care administration students and practitioners. CFD also maintains a library on death and dying and offers a speakers' bureau.

PUBLICATIONS: *Concern for Dying—Newsletter* and reports on developments in legislation, case law, and professional perspectives related to death, dying, and decision making. A living will appropriate to the requirements of each state is available free upon request.

Domestic Policy Council (DPC)
Old Executive Office Building, Room 231
The White House
Washington, DC 20500
(202) 456-6722

DPC advises the president on domestic and social policy. Members of the council include the attorney general; the secretaries of the interior, health and human services, housing and urban development, energy, education, and veterans affairs; the director of the Office of Management and Budget; and the administrator of the Environmental Protection Agency.

PUBLICATIONS: Occasionally reports are made available to the public through the Government Printing Office, but most information generated by DPC is confidential.

Forum for Health Care Planning
1101 Connecticut Avenue, NW, Suite 700
Washington, DC 20036
(202) 857-1162

This organization draws its members from senior-level executives, planners, consultants, architects, and other leaders in health care organizations such as hospitals, HMOs, universities, and ambulatory-care programs. Not a lobbying organization, the forum provides an opportunity for members to examine critical issues in ways that consider values. It holds the conviction that better planning and decision making in health care must deal not only with what is practical, but also with what is right.

PUBLICATIONS: *Forum News,* a quarterly newsletter.

Foundation for Hospice and Homecare (FHH)
519 C Street, NE
Washington, DC 20002-5809
(202) 547-6586

Founded in 1985, FHH promotes high standards of patient care for hospice and home-care services, with particular emphasis on the needs of the dying, the disabled, the disadvantaged, and the elderly. FHH also conducts research related to health services, aging, and social policies and develops and promotes innovative and efficient alternatives to current health and social policies. It promotes the development of a comprehensive continuum of health care and seeks to reverse negative stereotypes associated with age and physical impairment.

PUBLICATIONS: *Directory of Accredited Homemaker-Home Health Aide Services, Foundation News, All About Homecare—A Consumer's Guide,* and educational manuals.

Group Health Association of America, Inc. (GHAA)
1129 Twentieth Street, NW, Suite 600
Washington, DC 20036
(202) 778-3200

GHAA has represented the HMO industry since 1959 and is the largest trade group for health maintenance organizations. The group provides legislative representation, legal counsel, educational programs, research and analysis, library services, publications, and forums to its members. At the end of 1989, some 591 HMOs served 34.7 million people nationwide.

PUBLICATIONS: *National Directory of HMOs, HMO Industry Profile, HMO Managers Letter, HMO Magazine,* numerous research briefs, and several legislative and regulatory digests.

The Hastings Center
255 Elm Road
Briarcliff Manor, NY 10510
(914) 762-8500

Founded in 1969, the Hastings Center provides a forum for the discussion of difficult moral issues. Activities include research, education, and consultation. The center's fields of interest include ethics in law, medicine, science, philosophy, and religion. Present studies on ethical issues are related to aging, AIDS, care of the dying and termination of treatment, chronic illness, artificial reproduction, genetic screening, rehabilitative medicine, and justice in health care delivery. Through the Hastings Center, hundreds of universities have started courses in medical and professional ethics. Memberships are available.

PUBLICATIONS: The *Hastings Center Report, IRB: A Review of Human Subjects Research,* and books produced by the center's research groups. The *Hastings Center Report Index* provides an annual listing of articles published, indexed by both author and subject.

Health and Human Services Department
200 Independence Avenue, SW
Washington, DC 20201
(202) 619-0257

This major department of the federal government includes a number of agencies. The Health Care Financing Administration, for example, administers Medicaid and Medicare, while Prepaid Health Care sets national policies for HMOs and competitive medical plans.

Health Insurance Association of America (HIAA)
1025 Connecticut Avenue, NW
Washington, DC 20036-3998
(202) 223-7780

Founded in 1956, HIAA is the trade association that represents 350 commercial health insurance companies. Its members insure 90 million Americans—almost one-third of the population. A major lobbying organization, HIAA also provides educational programs, conferences, and information for its members.

PUBLICATIONS: Research bulletins, reports, and consumer publications. Of particular interest are the *1989 Source Book of Health Insurance Data* and the *HIAA Health Trends Chart Book 1989.*

Health Security Action Council (HSAC)
1757 N Street, NW
Washington, DC 20036
(202) 223-9685

Founded in 1969, HSAC works to increase grass-roots support for national health insurance and progressive health plans through publicity and education. The organization conducts surveys on the effects of federal legislative actions on state and local health programs. HSAC is affiliated with the Committee for National Health Insurance.

PUBLICATIONS: Brochures related to national health insurance, including "Health Security Partnership," a specific legislative proposal to restructure the U.S. health care system.

The Healthcare Forum
830 Market Street
San Francisco, CA 94102
(415) 421-8810

The Healthcare Forum is a national nonprofit educational association whose members include hospitals, health care systems, universities, corporations, suppliers, individuals, alternative providers, and others. Founded in 1927 as the Association of Western Hospitals, the forum provides an executive education series for members.

PUBLICATIONS: *Healthcare Forum Journal, The Forum Report,* and *The Source Book.* The latter publication lists more than 50,000 health care managers and suppliers by name and title.

Hemlock Society
P.O. Box 11830
Eugene, OR 97440-3900
(503) 342-5748

This nonprofit organization has over 36,000 members nationally. The Hemlock Society seeks to provide a climate of public opinion that is tolerant of the right of the terminally ill to end their own lives in a planned manner. It does not encourage suicide for any primary emotional, traumatic, or financial reasons in the absence of terminal illness and approves of the work of those involved in suicide prevention.

PUBLICATIONS: *Hemlock Quarterly Newsletter,* plus a number of books on the right to die with dignity and how to write a living will.

Intergovernmental Health Policy Project (IHPP)
2011 I Street, NW, Suite 200
Washington, DC 20006
(202) 872-1445

The Intergovernmental Health Policy Project at George Washington University is the only university-based program in the United States concentrating its research exclusively on the health laws and programs of the 50 states. IHPP provides information to state executive officials, legislators, legislative staff, and others about important developments in other states. IHPP also helps federal officials identify innovative state health programs and specific state problems.

PUBLICATIONS: *State Health Notes, State Health Reports,* and *Intergovernmental AIDS Reports* newsletters, plus an extensive list of research monographs and surveys on legislation regarding various aspects of health care.

InterStudy
5715 Christmas Lake Road
P.O. Box 458
Excelsior, MN 55331-0458
(612) 474-1176

InterStudy is a nonprofit research, education, and consulting organization that studies and develops models of health care delivery and financing. Founded in 1973, its research covers a wide range of topics, with particular emphasis on HMO growth and development, competition in health care, long-term care for the aging, and analysis of public health care policies.

PUBLICATIONS: *The InterStudy Edge,* a quarterly report on the growth of HMOs, and numerous articles, reports, surveys, and books.

Kaiser Family Foundation
Quadrus
2400 Sand Hill Road
Menlo Park, CA 94025
(415) 854-9400

With assets of approximately $400 million, the Kaiser Family Foundation is one of the nation's largest and most active foundations in the field of health. In recent years, the foundation has focused its resources on health promotion and disease prevention, the development of techniques to better assess the outcomes of medical practice, efforts to improve primary-care services in South Africa, and efforts to increase the participation of minorities in the health professions in the United States.

Kennedy Institute of Ethics
Georgetown University
Washington, DC 20057
(202) 687-3885

The Kennedy Institute of Ethics was founded in 1971 as a research and teaching center of Georgetown University. It was established to offer moral perspectives on major contemporary policy issues. The approach is interdisciplinary, with an emphasis on bioethical questions. Course work, research, and publications are offered, as well as library and information services. Memberships in the Kennedy Institute are available.

PUBLICATIONS: *New Titles in Bioethics* (11 times a year) and an annual *Bioethics Thesaurus.* The *International Directory of Bioethics Organizations* is also available. Through the Kennedy Institute, the National Reference Center for Bioethics Literature has the world's largest library collection related to ethical issues in medicine and biomedical research. For information, call (800) MED-ETHX.

National Association of Counties
440 First Street, NW
Washington, DC 20001
(202) 393-6226

This association promotes federal understanding of county government's role in providing, funding, and overseeing health care services at the local level. The group is interested in such issues as indigent health care, Medicaid and Medicare, prevention of and services for AIDS, long-term care, mental health, maternal and child health, and traditional public health programs.

PUBLICATIONS: *CHR (County Health Report)* newsletter.

National Association of Health Underwriters (NAHU)
1000 Connecticut Avenue, NW, Suite 1111
Washington, DC 20036
(202) 223-5533

Founded in 1930, this nonprofit organization has a membership of over 10,000 health insurance professionals. NAHU actively lobbies on behalf of the health insurance industry and promotes education, legislation, regulation, and practices that are in the best interest of the health insurance industry. Major concerns of the organization include national health insurance, taxation of employee benefits, and long-term-care insurance. NAHU provides continuing education for its members.

PUBLICATIONS: *The Health Insurance Underwriter.*

National Association for Home Care (NAHC)
519 C Street, NE
Washington, DC 20002
(202) 547-7424

NAHC is the trade association that represents home health agencies, hospices, and homemaker-home health aide organizations. Members are primarily corporations or other organizational entities. The organization was founded in 1982 through a merger of the National Association of Home Health Agencies and the Council of Home Health Agencies/Community Health Services. In addition to representing its members before Congress, regulatory agencies, and the media, NAHC provides educational opportunities, information services, and other benefits to members.

PUBLICATIONS: *Caring Magazine* and *Homecare News*. Other publications cover management, quality assurance, public relations, research and data, and other topics of interest to home health care professionals.

National Committee for Quality Health Care
1500 K Street, NW, Suite 360
Washington, DC 20005
(202) 347-5731

This committee is a broad-based coalition of nonprofit and for-profit hospitals and hospital systems, HMOs, pharmaceutical corporations, and other professional firms that supply goods and services to the health care industry. It serves as a forum for educating the public about trends affecting access to quality health care and for developing solutions consistent with a strong private-sector health care delivery system. The committee is the only health care trade group that has a membership base of leaders from all sectors of the health care industry. It provides special reports in critical industrywide issues and maintains a health care information center for members.

PUBLICATIONS: *Critical Condition: America's Health Care in Jeopardy, An American Health Strategy: Ensuring the Availability of Quality Health Care, United States versus Canadian Health Care, Quality Bulletin,* and *Quality Outlook.*

National Conference of State Legislatures (NCSL)
1560 Broadway, Suite 700
Denver, CO 80202
(303) 830-2200

NCSL was created in 1975 by the merger of three organizations that served or represented state legislatures. It is a nonpartisan organization that seeks to improve the quality and effectiveness of state legislatures and foster interstate communication and cooperation. NCSL provides a database of state legislators, top state executive branch officials, and senior legislative staff. Although NCSL's information services are directed at legislators, they are a valuable resource for researchers trying to identify the individuals involved in making decisions regarding health care in a particular state. NCSL can also help identify which states are passing legislation on specific health care issues.

PUBLICATIONS: *Critical Issues,* its current catalog, lists ten publications in the health care field. Also offered is the *Index to State Policy Reports* in *LIGISNET,* a comprehensive index to state policy publications. NCSL also publishes books, periodicals, state-federal issue briefs, updates on laws, and *State Legislatures,* a journal published ten times a year. NCSL also provides videotapes and audiotapes. Although fees are charged for these materials, most state legislators are members of NCSL; they may be willing to provide access to materials for their constituents.

National Council on the Aging, Inc. (NCOA)
600 Maryland Avenue, SW, West Wing 100
Washington, DC 20024
(202) 479-6605
(800) 424-9046

Founded in 1950, this organization is made up of professionals who provide services to older persons. It is active in advocacy and policy and program development on every issue affecting the quality of life for older Americans, including health promotion, senior housing, adult day care, senior centers, literacy, fitness, and retirement planning.

PUBLICATIONS: *Perspective on Aging, NCOA Networks,* and *Abstracts in Social Gerontology: Current Literature on Aging.* A publications catalog is also available.

National Council on Patient Information and Education
666 Eleventh Street, NW, Suite 810
Washington, DC 20001
(202) 347-6711

The National Council on Patient Information and Education was established in 1982. It is a nonprofit coalition of organizations committed to improving communications between health care professionals and patients about prescription medicines so that patients are better prepared to work with their health care providers and to follow their medication therapies safely and effectively. The council's objectives are to increase consumer awareness of the right to know and the need to know about prescription medicines and to increase professional awareness of the need to give more and better information on drug therapy.

PUBLICATIONS: A catalog of publications is available on request. Information booklets are geared to reach children and teenagers as well as older adults.

National Health Care Anti-Fraud Association (NHCAA)
1255 Twenty-third Street, NW, Suite 850
Washington, DC 20037-1174
(202) 659-5955

Founded in 1985, this association of private insurance carriers seeks to improve prevention, detection, and civil and criminal prosecution of health care fraud. NHCAA promotes information sharing among members, engages in public education, offers training, and serves in an advisory capacity to industry, regulatory, and legislative bodies. Members include private insurance carriers, Blue Cross and Blue Shield organizations, self-insured corporations, and federal and state regulatory and law-enforcement agencies.

PUBLICATIONS: *NHCAA News,* a quarterly newsletter with association news and updates on developments in the national effort against health care fraud.

National Health Council
350 Fifth Avenue, Suite 1118
New York, NY 10118
(212) 268-8900

This private, nonprofit association of national organizations was founded in 1920 as a clearinghouse and cooperative effort for voluntary health agencies. Membership encompasses professional and other membership associations, health-related nonprofit agencies, business corporations, and federal government agencies. The council's mission is to enable its member organizations to work together effectively to promote the health of all Americans with a strong sense of human concern, especially for vulnerable people. It seeks to stimulate greater public awareness of health and health-related concerns and to strengthen cooperative efforts among health-related private-sector organizations and between the private and governmental sectors.

PUBLICATIONS: *Health Groups in Washington: A Directory; Congress and Health; Long-Term Care: In Search of National Policy;* and *Long-Term Care: Economic Impacts and Financing Dilemmas.*

National Health Information Center
P.O. Box 1133
Washington, DC 20013-1133
(800) 336-4797
(301) 565-4167 in Maryland

A service of the Office of Disease Prevention and Health Promotion of the U.S. Public Health Service, the center is a health information referral organization. It puts people with health questions in touch with those organizations that are best able to answer them. Office hours are between 9 A.M. and 5 P.M. eastern standard time.

PUBLICATIONS: For a minimal handling fee, the center makes available a number of government publications. Topics range from policy questions to school health education to health in the workplace.

National Health Policy Forum (NHPF)
George Washington University
2001 I Street, NW, Suite 200
Washington, DC 20006
(202) 872-1390

The National Health Policy Forum is a nonpartisan educational program serving congressional, White House, and executive agency specialists in health affairs, as well as others across the country. Its purpose is to offer the nation's federal health policymakers ready access to the most knowledgeable people in other levels of government, the health professions, business, labor, academe, and consumer groups. More than 500 people who occupy influential policy positions within Congress and the executive branch participate in the forum. It serves as the principal vehicle through which decision makers forge the personal acquaintances and understanding necessary for cooperation among government agencies and between government and the private sector. NHPF offers seminars and briefings, conducts site visits, and provides numerous publications. The forum's Intergovernmental Health Policy Project at George Washington University is the only university-based program in the country concentrating its research efforts exclusively on the health laws and programs of the 50 states.

PUBLICATIONS: *State Health Notes, State Health Reports,* and various briefs related to health care. Of particular interest is a December 1989 background issue brief, *The Pharmaceutical Industry.*

National Institute of Mental Health (NIMH)
U.S. Department of Health and Human Services
Public Health Service
Alcohol, Drug Abuse, and Mental Health Administration
5600 Fishers Lane, Room 15C-05
Rockville, MD 20857
(301) 443-4513

The National Institute of Mental Health is the largest scientific institute in the world with a primary focus on mental disorders. In addition to employing nearly 600 scientists in its own research program, NIMH supports over 90 percent of the nation's research on mental health. It also collaborates with other federal and state agencies, as well as national and local organizations, to promote effective mental health programs. NIMH provides technical assistance to states and localities in the planning and maintenance of sound activities for the care and treatment of the mentally ill.

PUBLICATIONS: A list of publications includes materials written for both mental health specialists and the general public. Specific mental disorders are covered, as well as mental health administration, evaluation, policy, and services.

National Institutes of Health (NIH)
U.S. Department of Health and Human Services
Division of Public Information
Office of Communications
Bethesda, MD 20892
(301) 496-4143

Beginning as a one-room lab in 1887, NIH has evolved into one of the world's foremost biomedical research centers. As the federal focal point for health research, it strives to uncover new knowledge that will lead to better health for everyone. NIH conducts research in hundreds of laboratories; supports research of nonfederal scientists in universities, medical schools, hospitals, and research institutions in the United States and abroad; trains research investigators; and fosters biomedical communication. Also located on its grounds in Bethesda, Maryland, are the Warren Grant Magnuson Clinical Center and the National Library of Medicine.

PUBLICATIONS: *NIH Almanac* (pertinent facts about NIH), *NIH Data Book,* and *NIH Publications List.* Publications listed are generally free to the public and tend to be disease specific, such as "Dental Tips for Diabetics." The topics are categorized for the general public or for health professionals or as technical reports.

National Leadership Coalition for Health Care Reform
555 Thirteenth Street, NW
Washington, DC 20004
(202) 637-6830

Formed in 1986 by a group of concerned citizens to address the three major problems of cost, quality, and access to health care, the National Leadership Coalition on Health Care proposes a major restructuring of the nation's health care system. Formerly known as the National Leadership Commission on Health Care, the coalition seeks universal access to a basic level of health services. The coalition is committed to developing a new public-private partnership and a systematic reform plan for the nation's health care system.

National Library of Medicine (NLM)
8600 Rockville Pike
Bethesda, MD 20894
(301) 496-6308 general inquiries/publications
(301) 496-6095 reference services

NLM is the world's largest research library in a single scientific and professional field. It collects materials exhaustively in all major areas of the health sciences. The current collection stands at approximately 4.5 million items. MEDLARS®, the library's computer-based medical literature analysis and retrieval system, provides rapid access to NLM's store of biomedical information.

National Mental Health Association (NMHA)
1021 Prince Street
Alexandria, VA 22314-2971
(703) 684-7722
(800) 969-NMHA

This is the nation's only citizens' volunteer advocacy organization concerned with all aspects of mental health and mental illness. With over 600 affiliates across the country, NMHA works to meet this challenge through education, research, services, and advocacy on a local, state, and national level. The organization promotes state and federal legislation to develop funding for mental health services and to protect patients' rights. It also encourages research funding to uncover causes of and treatments for mental illnesses. NMHA acts as a clearinghouse for information and refers people to agencies or support groups with specific knowledge about a particular illness.

PUBLICATIONS: *Focus,* a quarterly newsletter, and *Legislative Alert,* which tracks bills affecting mental health through Congress. A booklet of publications offers general information on mental illness, advocacy resources, mental health policy resources, resource development, and other topics.

National Research Council
2101 Constitution Avenue
Washington, DC 20418
(202) 334-2000

The National Research Council is the working arm of the National Academy of Sciences and the National Academy of Engineering; it carries out most of the studies done in their names. The council is not a membership organization; its mission is to provide most of the services to governmental agencies and Congress that are undertaken by the National Academy of Sciences and the National Academy of Engineering in their roles as advisers to the federal government. This work is done primarily through its committee structure, which calls upon a wide cross section of leading scientists and other professionals, who serve on its committees without pay. In a typical year, there are a total of more than 1,000 committees with approximately 10,000 professionals volunteering their time to serve on them. The Institute of Medicine, operating through the National Research Council, responds to questions relating to public health policy, care, research, and education.

PUBLICATIONS: Numerous reports.

National Wellness Institute
South Hall
1319 Fremont Street
Stevens Point, WI 54481-3899
(715) 346-2172

A nonprofit organization, the National Wellness Institute was founded in 1977. The 1,500-member National Wellness Association, which is a division of the National Wellness Institute, provides professional training and development through its week-long National Wellness Conference, which is held every summer in Stevens Point, Wisconsin. Members are professionals involved in wellness programs in hospital- and clinic-based programs as well as work-site, campus, and school programs. The association also provides information and consultation services and distributes wellness products, primarily health assessment tools.

PUBLICATIONS: *Wellness Resource Catalog* and *Wellness Management Newsletter.*

Office of Technology Assessment (OTA)
Health and Life Sciences Division
600 Pennsylvania Avenue, SE
U.S. Congress
Washington, DC 20510-8025
(202) 224-8713

The Office of Technology Assessment acts on requests from Senate and House committees for research studies on general health care issues, including health care technologies and the cost and quality of child, adolescent, and elderly health care. This government agency is a good resource for up-to-date statistics.

People's Medical Society
462 Walnut Street
Allentown, PA 18102
(215) 770-1670

With over 80,000 members, the People's Medical Society is the United States' largest consumer health advocacy organization. The nonprofit organization's goals are to make medical consumers better informed, by offering information about the health care system that is not normally available, and to reform the health care system to be more responsive to consumers. The organization is founded on the premise that the existing health care system is too expensive, too impersonal, and too unwilling to concentrate on preventive medicine.

PUBLICATIONS: *People's Medical Society Newsletter,* a bimonthly publication providing information on a variety of topics, including how to avoid unnecessary treatment, how to choose a doctor, and how to save money on medical bills. It also includes exposés of unethical and incompetent practitioners and wrongdoing in organized medicine. The society also publishes health action kits, health bulletins, and books about health care.

Public Citizen
P.O. Box 19404
Washington, DC 20036
(202) 872-0320

Public Citizen is a nonprofit membership organization representing consumer interests through lobbying, litigation, research, and publications. Since its founding by Ralph Nader in 1971, Public Citizen has fought for consumer rights, many of them involving health care. The organization is active in Congress, the courts, government agencies, and the media. It has won 12 cases before the U.S. Supreme Court, including ones requiring disclosure of prescription drug price information.

PUBLICATIONS: *Health Letter,* a monthly newsletter providing information on such critical health questions as how to choose safe hospitals and affordable quality medical care, how to avoid food contaminated with carcinogens, how to gain access to medical records, and how to save money by purchasing generic drugs. Public Citizen also publishes an extensive list of available reports, articles, and testimony on health-related topics.

The Rand Corporation
1700 Main Street
P.O. Box 2138
Santa Monica, CA 90406-2138
(213) 393-0411

The Rand Corporation is a private, nonprofit institution engaged in research and analysis of matters affecting national security and the public welfare. It offers doctoral degree programs at the Rand Graduate School. Areas of research include applied science and technology, arms control, civil and criminal justice, defense, health, and human resources.

PUBLICATIONS: A booklet of publications lists subscription libraries across the nation that have Rand publications in their collections. Although many of Rand's books do not relate to health care, a bibliography of selected publications lists those related to health care costs and coverage. The newsletter *Rand Research Review* comes out three times a year, but most issues focus on topics other than health care.

The Robert Wood Johnson Foundation
P.O. Box 2316
Princeton, NJ 08543-2316
(609) 452-8701

The Robert Wood Johnson Foundation is one of the world's largest private, independent philanthropies devoted to improving health and medical care. The foundation's areas of interest currently include vulnerable populations, specific diseases, and broad national health issues. It is a significant resource for information concerning the health care crisis. Since the foundation's inception in 1972, it has awarded over a billion dollars in grant funds for projects judged to be likely to improve the health and health care of Americans. Since 1974, the foundation has continuously supported Georgetown University as an information clearinghouse about health policies and programs at the state and local levels.

PUBLICATIONS: *Helping Shape the Nation's Health Care System* (a report on the foundation's program activities from 1972 through 1989), *Advances Newsletter,* and numerous special reports.

Society for Health and Human Values
6728 Old McLean Village Drive
McLean, VA 22101
(703) 556-9222

The Society for Health and Human Values promotes the inclusion of humanities disciplines in the curricula of health professional schools and presents programs dealing with human values, humanities, and medical ethics. The society's 810 members are drawn from many disciplines, such as medicine, law, education, and philosophy. It seeks to foster an awareness of ethical and humanistic values in the training of health practitioners through computer networking among members, developing handbooks, cataloging curriculum resources, and identifying foreign travel support.

PUBLICATIONS: *Bulletin of the Society for Health and Human Values, Medical Humanities Review,* and numerous professional publications related to the teaching of ethics in medicine.

University of Minnesota Center for Biomedical Ethics
Box 33 UNHC
420 Delaware Street, SE
Minneapolis, MN 55455
(612) 625-4917

The mission of the Center for Biomedical Ethics is to advance and disseminate knowledge concerning ethical issues in health care and the life sciences. It conducts interdisciplinary research, offers educational programs and courses, fosters public discussion and debate through community-service activities, and assists in the formulation of public policy. In 1989, its staff granted interviews and responded to requests from more than 500 media organizations.

PUBLICATIONS: Research project reports and cassette tapes of lectures are available; fees vary, so write for the publication list. Of particular interest to those researching the health care crisis is the report, *Rethinking Medical Morality: The Ethical Implications of Changes in Health Care Organization, Delivery, and Financing* ($10.00).

Washington Business Group on Health (WBGH)
777 North Capitol Street, NE, Suite 800
Washington, DC 20002
(202) 408-9320

Founded in 1974, this nonprofit national health policy and research organization gives major employers a voice in the formulation of health care policy. Membership includes 180 employers, many of them large nationally known corporations. In addition to its public policy function, WBGH includes several institutes that conduct research, identify trends, collect and disseminate information, and provide long-range planning and analysis on the economic and social issues confronting employers.

PUBLICATIONS: *Together on Aging,* a quarterly newsletter, and *Business and Health,* a monthly magazine published in conjunction with American Health Consultants, Inc. Other publications include numerous reports, testimonies, and conference transcripts.

For a more extensive list of organizations related to health care, see *Encyclopedia of Associations* (New York: Gale Research Inc. ISBN 0-8103-491-6 [vol. 1]; 0-8103-7422-6 [vol. 1, part 2]). Published annually, this extensive reference in three volumes includes details on more than 22,000 organizations headquartered in the United States.

6

References in Print

THE FOLLOWING IS A HIGHLY SELECTIVE LIST of reference works, including handbooks, yearbooks, bibliographies, significant books and monographs, and periodicals. Scholarly works as well as government and privately produced reports are included. The more popularly oriented works range from the theoretical to the practical. Although the overall emphasis of this list of references is on policy and the health care crisis in general, widely varying viewpoints are represented and the annotations are unavoidably subjective. For these reasons, it is important to note that the reader ultimately must decide the validity of any given point of view.

In order to stay abreast of the rapidly changing health field and to make this book as current as possible, the majority of the listed references was published in 1985 or later. (Prices and ISBNs are included where available.)

Yearbooks

American Statistics Index (ASI). Washington, DC: Congressional Information Service, 1973–. Annual. $2,220.

This annual comprehensive guide and index to the statistical publications of the U.S. government is available at libraries that house federal government documents. Monthly supplements continually update this reference series, and there are also annual cumulative indexes. ASI consists of two companion volumes: The first is an index, and the second is abstracts. Extensive listings in each series relate to health care, medical care, medical costs, survey results, and so forth. Individual items not available at libraries may be ordered from the U.S. Government Printing Office.

Health, United States. Hyattsville, MD: U.S. Department of Health and Human Services, Public Health Service, 1975–. Annual. $19.00.

This report on the health status of the nation is submitted annually by the Health and Human Services Department to the president and Congress. The annual report presents data to measure and evaluate the progress of the nation's health and recent trends in the health care sector. The statistics included fall into four major categories: health status and determinants, utilization of health resources, health care resources, and health care expenditures. The 1989 report also contains the fourth triennial *Prevention Profile* compiled by the National Center for Health Statistics, Centers for Disease Control.

NIH Almanac. Bethesda, MD: Division of Public Information, 1970–. Free.

Each year the National Institutes of Health (NIH) publishes pertinent facts about the federal government's principal biomedical research agency. It provides a reference source of NIH's 13 research institutes and 4 divisions, the National Library of Medicine, the Clinical Center, the National Center of Nursing Research, and the John E. Fogarty International Center for Advanced Study in the Health Sciences. The yearbook includes historical data, currently funded programs with grant amounts, and biographical sketches of current directors. To receive a *free* copy of the almanac, write to NIH, Bethesda, MD 20892.

1989 Health Care Legislation. Denver, CO: National Conference of State Legislatures, 1990. 238p. Annual. $15.00. ISBN 1-55516-692-X.

This publication is the seventh in a series summarizing significant health care laws passed by the 50 states each year. Over 1,000 acts are included, covering topics ranging from medical ethics to health insurance and medical malpractice. The emphasis is on health care financing and cost-containment legislation, but other important health issues are also included. Although the citations are brief, identification numbers are provided so the reader can request further information from the appropriate state.

Statistical Abstract of the United States. Washington, DC: U.S. Department of Commerce, U.S. Bureau of the Census, 1978–. Annual. $34.00; $28.00 (paper).

This large annual compilation of statistics on everything from human services to national defense includes a large section on health and nutrition. It is available at most public libraries.

Bibliographies and Directories

American Hospital Association Guide to the Health Care Field. Chicago, IL: American Hospital Association, 1974–. $150.00.

This annual directory lists registered hospitals; health care systems; international, national, and regional organizations; state organizations and agencies; and health care providers such as freestanding ambulatory-care centers, health maintenance organizations (HMOs), and freestanding substance-abuse and psychiatric facilities.

Health Groups in Washington: A Directory. 1989 ed. New York: National Health Council, 1980–. 170p. $15.00. ISBN 0-929852-01-X.

The tenth edition of this directory contains over 660 listings of health and health-related organizations in the Washington, D.C., area. Each entry lists the name, address, and phone number of the organization, as well as the names and titles of key contacts. Extensive subject and name indexes are provided.

International Directory of Bioethics Organizations. Washington, DC: National Reference Center for Bioethics Literature, Kennedy Institute of Ethics, 1987. 21p. Free.

Bioethics organizations from 22 states and 25 foreign countries are listed. Listings include addresses, telephone numbers, and the program directors.

National Health Directory, 1990. Rockville, MD: Aspen Publishers, 1990. 600p. $89.00. ISBN 0-8342-0171-2; ISSN 0147-2771.

This directory is a guide for lobbyists and others who need to know who directs and carries out health care legislation. More than just a listing of government agencies and personnel involved in health care issues, the directory also includes federal and state legislators and their staffs.

Watts, Tim J. **The Pharmaceutical Industry: Regulation and Liability.** Valparaiso, IN: Vance Bibliographies, 1988. 27p. $7.50. ISBN 1-55590-708-3.

Although the pharmaceutical industry plays a major role in health care in the United States, few recent books have been written on the subject.

This bibliography is a valuable reference to recent articles written about the pharmaceutical industry.

Studies, Surveys, and Commission Reports

Aaron, Henry J., and William B. Schwartz. **The Painful Prescription: Rationing Hospital Care.** Washington, DC: The Brookings Institution, 1984. 161p. Index. $26.95; $9.95 (paper). ISBN 0-8157-0034-2; 0-8157-0033-4 (paper).

This study by the Brookings Institution examines the British health care system in depth. It uses the British experience as the basis for drawing inferences about how Americans would respond to a sharp reduction of growth in medical spending. It concludes that the type of rationing prevalent in England would be unacceptable to most Americans for a number of reasons. Although this study is older than most listings in this bibliography, it is included because of the detailed explanation of how the British health care system works. As the health care crisis increases in the United States, the British system is often cited as an alternative model.

The Bristol-Myers Report: Medicine in the Next Century. New York: Louis Harris and Associates, 1987. Study number 86018. 206p.

Louis Harris and Associates surveyed 227 world-class scientists as part of a study to examine what their priorities and primary areas of medical research will be in the next century. Highlights of the report include the opinion that the new frontier for medical research is the fundamental understanding of cell mechanisms. Those surveyed also believe that the most important health problems in the West will be those stemming from an aging population. A majority (52 percent) see a cure for AIDS by the year 2010, and 40 percent of the scientists consider the lack of adequate funds and financial support to be their chief frustration. Expectations are also listed in the specific research areas of cancer, cardiovascular disease, nutrition, and medical implants.

The Environment of Medicine. Chicago, IL: American Medical Association, 1989. 87p. Members $20.00; nonmembers $50.00. ISBN 0-89970-346-1.

This detailed analysis of trends in the environment of medicine was prepared by the AMA Council on Long-Range Planning and Development. It discusses trends affecting medicine and major issues affecting health care. Many of the tables project trends into the year 2000; these are helpful for researchers frustrated by government statistics, which are often several years old. Of particular interest are changing roles in the health care sector and the conclusions and implications drawn about the future of health care.

For the Health of a Nation: A Shared Responsibility. Ann Arbor, MI: Health Administration Press, 1989. 206p. Bibliography. $23.00. ISBN 0-910701-51-2.

This report of the National Leadership Commission on Health Care, 1986–1989, is reviewed in Chapter 4.

Health Care in the 1990s: Trends and Strategies. Chicago, IL: Arthur Anderson and Company and the American College of Hospital Administrators, 1984. 43p.

Arthur Anderson and Company, an international accounting and consulting firm, and the American College of Hospital Administrators conducted a study to determine the consensus of health care experts concerning the future direction of the health care system. This survey of 1,000 experts throughout the health care field assesses the trends and strategies shaping the industry today. Significant changes are predicted for hospitals, physicians, and patients. Among the predictions: that malpractice awards will be limited, preferred provider organizations (PPOs) and HMOs will increase their market shares fivefold, more outpatient and urgent-care centers will compete with hospitals, investor-owned hospitals will increase, and more nonhospital providers will compete for capital. The report includes numerous charts and graphs, which make the statistics easy to understand.

Medical Professional Liability and the Delivery of Obstetrical Care, vols. 1 and 2. Washington, DC: National Academy Press, 1989. Vol. 1, 240p.; vol. 2, 238p. Bibliography. Index. $29.95. ISBN 0-309-03982-7 (vol. 1). $35.00. ISBN 0-399-03986-X (vol. 2).

This interdisciplinary review sponsored by the Institute of Medicine reflects rising concern among medical professionals about the effects of the liability situation on the delivery of and access to obstetrical care. Volume 1 contains results of surveys conducted by the Institute of Medicine, while volume 2 contains commissioned papers by a broad range of interdisciplinary professionals. The papers were presented at a research symposium on 20 June 1988. The study reaches no consensus on the causes of the medical professional liability controversy, except that experts agree that no single factor is responsible.

President's Commission for the Study of Ethical and Legal Problems in Medicine and Biomedical and Behavioral Research. Washington, DC: U.S. Government Printing Office, 1983. Pr 40.8: Et 3/SU6.

This extensive study is reviewed in Chapter 4.

Reforming Health Care: A Market Prescription. New York: Research and Policy Committee of the Committee for Economic Development, 1987. ISBN 0-87186-784-2; 0-87186-084-8 (paper).

This study was conducted by the Research and Policy Committee of the Committee for Economic Development, an independent research and educational organization of over 200 business executives and educators. The causes of the health care crisis are reviewed, and reform is proposed based on market incentives. The study is business oriented, with reform defined as strengthening the economy and ensuring a high standard of living. It identifies the three major problems facing health care as cost, access, and quality. Faulty payment systems are examined as contributing to cost escalation, and the extent of government involvement in health care is examined in detail. Of particular interest is a section that covers ways to stimulate pharmaceutical innovation, a factor not taken into account by most books scrutinizing the health care crisis.

Handbook

O'Connell, Jeffrey. **Ending the Lottery: A Consumer Proposal for Medical Malpractice Reform.** Washington, DC: HALT, Inc., 1987. 18p. ISBN 0-910073-11-2.

This booklet was published by HALT, a nonprofit organization that seeks to improve the U.S. legal system. It succinctly summarizes the inadequacies and inequities in the U.S. tort system of law, concluding that the system cannot be expected to solve the medical malpractice crisis. The fairness of no-fault and fair-trade reform proposals is evaluated. The author proposes a new reform, "neo-no-fault," and discusses the pros and cons of this system.

Books

General

Abramson, Leonard. **Healing Our Health Care System.** New York: Grove Weidenfeld, 1990. 143p. Index. $18.95. ISBN 0-8021-1257-9.

This examination of our health care system is highly critical of many sectors of the medical community. Hospitals, physicians, insurance companies, HMOs, the government, and business are all cited for failures to manage well and keep costs down. The strengths of this book are frank criticism and proposed solutions. The chapters explaining how HMOs and indemnity insurance companies work are particularly valuable for the lay reader; however, as the head of a large HMO organization, the author does demonstrate a strong bias against non-profit health organizations. Chapter 14 features "Typical Questions, Some Untypical Answers," and up-to-date statistics are sprinkled liberally throughout the book.

Bergthold, Linda. **Purchasing Power in Health: Business, the State, and Health Care Politics.** New Brunswick, NJ: Rutgers University Press, 1990. 213p. Bibliography. Index. $37.00. ISBN 0-8135-1487-8.

This book presents a well-documented argument that business has had a significant effect on health care politics in the period from 1969 to 1988. It describes the participation of business in health policy formation, the organizations that business mobilized to promote its interests, and the types of policies that business interests have promoted. In this context, "business" is used to describe the activities and the economic interests of large corporations, which are major purchasers of medical care services for their employees. This complex volume explains in detail how business became involved in health care through the formation of coalitions, associations, and lobbying groups; through advisory roles to state and federal governments; and through direct participation in the legislative process. Although economically oriented, this book will be useful to the lay reader interested in the role of business in influencing the health care system.

Califano, Joseph A., Jr. **America's Health Care Revolution: Who Lives? Who Dies?** New York: Random House, 1986. 241p. Bibliography. Index. $17.95; $9.95 (paper). ISBN 0-394-54291-6; 0-671-68371-3 (paper).

This book provides an overview of the U.S. health care system and how it evolved. As former secretary of the U.S. Department of Health, Education, and Welfare, the author is a recognized expert on the health industry. Startling points are made to jar the reader into reevaluating the traditional health care system. For example, this is a unique system in which doctors who cannot find things to do to patients do not get paid. The freedom-of-choice myth is dispelled: As long as doctors give patients no information on quality or price, how can there be freedom? Disparaging titles, such as calling hospitals the "Temples of Medicine Men" and doctors "Profitable Acolytes" should be overlooked. Even with its touch of sarcasm, this volume provides an excellent summary of the current health care crisis. It concludes with a discussion of what is possible in the future.

Coddington, Dean C., et al. **The Crisis in Health Care: Costs, Choices, and Strategies.** San Francisco: Jossey-Bass, Inc., 1990. 304p. Bibliography. Index. $30.95. ISBN 1-55542-273-X.

The health care industry has lost the ability to control costs, and present payment systems will have to change in the future. This excellent book examines the factors contributing to rising costs, identifies pressures for change, and discusses four scenarios of possible future payment systems. Cost shifting is identified as a major factor contributing to the rising cost of medical care. Cost shifting occurs when the cost of care provided to the uninsured or to those receiving deep discounts (HMOs, Medicaid, Medicare, and large employers) is not being fully reimbursed, and smaller firms and individuals are making up the difference. Another contributing factor to rising costs are the efforts of insurers and managed-care organizations trying to make up for underwriting losses. Continuing advances in medical technology also drive up costs.

Dougherty, Charles J. **American Health Care: Realities, Rights, and Reforms.** New York: Oxford University Press, 1988. 288p. Bibliography. Index. $29.95; $16.95 (paper). ISBN 0-19-505271-4; 0-19-505272-2 (paper).

This complex study is divided into three main parts: the performance of the present health care system, a defense of the concept of a moral right to health care, and the alternatives for reform of the system. Although parts one and three are informative and readable, the central section on the moral right to health care will challenge the average reader. However, an understanding of health care as a "right" is crucial to the final thesis that health care is not just another commodity or a field for corporate profit for the "medical-industrial complex." Health care should be a right, with the primary goal of the health system to provide an important public good. Reform of the U.S. health care system is stated as a necessity, but a variety of solutions are given, all with certain drawbacks.

Dutton, Diana B. **Worse than the Disease.** New York: Cambridge University Press, 1988. 528p. Bibliography. Index. $29.95; $14.95 (paper). ISBN 0-521-34023-3; 0-521-395577 (paper).

This book examines four case studies, including swine flu shots, use of the artificial heart, DES, and genetic engineering. Major mistakes were made because of the dominant role of technical and scientific experts in decision making. Suitable ways must be found to ensure that medical innovation responds to and reflects the interests of all sectors of society. The book also includes a list of the problems created by the cutbacks in public financing of health care in the 1980s. The professional and industrial interests that have a stake in government policy dominate economic markets, therefore dominating the political process. Our society must find a way to achieve broader public participation in deciding what direction health care takes in the future.

Feldstein, Paul J. **The Politics of Health Legislation: An Economic Perspective.** Ann Arbor, MI: Health Administration Press, 1988. 258p. Bibliographies. Index. $28.00. ISBN 0-910701-35-0 (paper).

This book examines the health care system from an economic and political perspective, demonstrating that legislative and regulatory outcomes are largely due to the self-interest of individuals, groups, or legislators. In the case of legislators, the primary self-interest is reelection, which leads to health care legislation limited to a short-term perspective. Intriguing analyses are given of the motives behind the lobbying power of such groups as the American Medical Association, the American Hospital Association, and groups representing the elderly. The effects of third-party payment and market competition on the health care system are also discussed. Although based on an economic and political point of view, the language in this insightful volume is understandable to the average reader. The book provides an unusual perspective on the causes of the health care crisis. The notes at the end of each chapter are extensive.

Ginzberg, Eli. **The Medical Triangle: Physicians, Politicians, and the Public.** Cambridge, MA: Harvard University Press, 1990. 314p. Bibliography. Index. $27.50. ISBN 0-674-56325-5.

A well-known health policy expert examines the issues surrounding the health care crisis in a historical, political, and professional context. This excellent, well-written book focuses on three sides of the medical triangle that have separate and sometimes conflicting goals: physicians, the government, and the public. A broad, well-balanced perspective is maintained throughout. The historical section of the book is a valuable summary of the numerous diverse factors that have propelled the health care system to its current volatile state. This destabilization of health care is examined in the final chapters through a focus on specific concerns, such as the infirmities of the aging population, nursing shortages, and unsuccessful attempts at cost containment.

Ginzberg, Eli, and Anna B. Dutka. **The Financing of Biomedical Research.** Baltimore: Johns Hopkins University Press, 1989. 144p. Bibliography. Index. $18.50. ISBN 0-8018-3813-4.

This volume assesses the enlarged role of biomedical research on the national scene. This role has transformed the education of physicians and the practice of medicine, has contributed to the strengthening of the U.S. pharmaceutical industry, and has speeded up the development of biotechnology. From 1940 to 1987, the estimated total expenditures for biomedical research grew fortyfold, in constant (inflation-adjusted) dollars. As the federal government began providing less money in the last two decades, philanthropy began contributing more, as it had in the pre–World War II era. In the concluding chapter, current problems in sustaining biomedical research are considered. These include inadequate funding for NIH, difficulties faced by academic health centers, and reduction in Medicare reimbursement for graduate medical education.

Hiatt, Howard H. **Medical Lifeboat: Will There Be Room for You in the Health Care System?** New York: Harper & Row, 1989. 252p. Bibliography. Index. $9.95. ISBN 0-06-091560-9 (paper). (An earlier version of this book was published in 1987 under the title *America's Health in the Balance: Choice or Chance,* ISBN 0-06-039063-8.)

Although the United States spends more per capita on health care than any other industrialized country, we are far from the healthiest nation in the world. We rank seventeenth worldwide in infant mortality and sixteenth in life expectancy. Costs are out of control and rising. The economic, medical, and social elements of the health care crisis are discussed from the broad point of view of the author, who is a physician, scientist, administrator, teacher, and medical statesman. Of particular interest are chapters that review the often-praised Canadian and British systems of nationalized health care. The book also includes a hypothetical model of a national health care system in the United States, which would incorporate the best aspects of these two systems.

Inlander, Charles B., Lowell S. Levin, and Ed Weiner, eds. **Medicine on Trial: Medical Mistakes and Incompetence in the Practice of Medicine Today.** Englewood Cliffs, NJ: Prentice Hall, 1988. 304p. Bibliography. Index. $18.95. ISBN 0-13-573544-0.

This exposé of the medical profession uncovers a variety of shocking abuses. Topics covered include the alleged high extent of drug abuse and alcoholism among medical professionals and the lack of sterile procedures. Faulty medical devices are criticized, as well as lethal inadvertent switching of drugs and other atrocities. Compiled by the directors of the People's Medical Society, the nation's largest consumer health organization, the book draws heavily from the medical profession's own studies. In addition to exposing abuses, the book calls for reform. Chapter 13 lists specific steps that could be taken to improve health care in the United States. The appendix provides the names and addresses of organizations where the aggrieved medical consumer can seek redress. Although it covers shocking topics, the book is written in a controlled, nonsensationalist style.

Jones, Rochelle. **The Supermeds.** New York: Charles Scribner's Sons, 1988. 261p. Bibliography. Index. $19.95. ISBN 0-684-18695-0.

This book postulates that the big business of medicine is endangering health care in the United States. It traces the rise of for-profit medical corporations, which have expanded from general hospitals into every health field. Believing that medicine is a product to be bought and sold, medical corporations are becoming increasingly powerful and are shaping the cost, kind, and quality of medical care offered to consumers. Taxpayers have unwittingly financed this corporate takeover and will pay once again in higher prices and lower-quality health care. The demise of the traditional sole practitioner is predicted, and considerable attention is given to the increasingly competitive medical arena. The book is scathingly critical of the effects of the profit motive on today's health care. It concludes that consumers must become their own advocates by taking control of the health care process.

Leder, Shelah, and Marilyn Moon, eds. **Changing America's Health Care System.** Glenview, IL: Scott, Foresman and Company, 1989. 164p. Bibliography. Index. ISBN 0-673-24895-X.

Written under the auspices of the American Association of Retired Persons (AARP), this collection of essays considers alternatives to our health care system. Each of the four specialists in health care agrees that a universal health care system is needed; however, they disagree on how to organize and finance such a system. The contributing authors respond to points made in one another's essays. In Chapter 8, AARP staff and members of the organization brainstorm on the ideas presented, concluding that something must be done to ensure universal and uniform health care. This concise book is particularly valuable in its presentation of possible solutions, since much of the literature about the health care crisis focuses on causes of the problem without proposing ways to solve it.

McKibbin, Richard C. **The Nursing Shortage and the 1990s: Realities and Remedies.** Kansas City, MO: American Nurses Association, 1990. 107p. Bibliography. $424.95. ISBN 1-55810-012-1.

This book explores the reasons behind the nursing shortage in the United States, which has been a national problem since 1986. It concludes that the shortage is the result of increasing demand. In the past, most proposed remedies for the shortage have focused on supply; this book, however, addresses such issues as how nurses are utilized and what tasks can be performed by others. As much as 50 percent of a nurse's time is spent on clerical, housekeeping, and other routine tasks that could be performed by others. In addition to proposing better utilization of professional skills, this volume proposes such remedies as more autonomy, better salaries and benefits, more educational opportunities, and better staffing patterns for nurses. Many excellent statistics, graphs, and charts that help define the nursing shortage are included.

Morris, Jonas. **Searching for a Cure: National Health Policy Considered.** New York: Pica Press, 1984. 235p. Bibliography. Index. $25.00. ISBN 0-87663-741-1.

This book examines the impact of federal policy upon the health care system and why that policy is what it is. It focuses on efforts over the past 20 years to start a program of national health insurance and on how and why those efforts have failed. However, since the campaign to institute national health insurance is only the most visible aspect of national health policy, the book attempts to reach beyond that to explore other major aspects of policymaking. Although older than most of the volumes listed in this chapter, this book is included because it provides an excellent historical review of the national health insurance controversy, from the New Deal years through the Reagan administration.

Rosenbaum, Edward E. **A Taste of My Own Medicine.** New York: Random House, 1988. 221p. $16.95. ISBN 0-394-56282-8.

A successful, nationally known physician gives a first-person account of his experience, late in his career, of being a patient himself. This humbling experience, as he is treated for throat cancer, gives him a new perspective on the physician-patient relationship. From his new position "on the other side of the bed," Dr. Rosenbaum is subjected to indignities and unthinking unkindness and experiences the fear, helplessness, and even rage familiar to most patients. This transformation of a doctor into a patients' advocate is more than a vividly evocative story. It also addresses the dehumanization of modern health care, which is often cited as one of the contributing factors to the health care crisis. This highly readable book also provides a sobering glimpse into the amount of guesswork still involved in medical diagnosis, the incompetencies of some care givers, and lapses of communication among health professionals.

Siegler, Mark, ed. **Medical Innovation and Bad Outcomes: Legal, Social, and Ethical Responses.** Ann Arbor, MI: Health Administration Press, 1987. 286p. Bibliography. Index. $32.00. ISBN 0-910701-15-6.

This collection of essays draws from experts in medicine, law, economics, statistics, history, philosophy, and public policy. It addresses the questions of who (if anyone) is responsible (morally and legally) and who (if anyone) is liable for compensating an individual who experiences a bad outcome that may have been caused by the use of a medical innovation. These essays clarify from various perspectives the conceptual issues of causation, moral responsibility, and legal responsibility that underlie efforts to change public policy regarding liability and compensation. Some of the essays are highly complex and technical, but many are comprehensible to the lay reader. Examples are drawn from well-known controversial bad outcomes from medical innovation, such as asbestosis, Agent Orange, DES, and the Dalkon shield.

Sorkin, Alan L. **Health Care and the Changing Economic Environment.** Lexington, MA: D. C. Heath and Company, 1986. 161p. Index. $20.00. ISBN 0-669-09016-6.

The impact of the changing economic environment on the nation's health care system is explored, with special attention given to the effect of increased competition and the growth of the for-profit segment of the health care industry. Health care trends are discussed, including rising costs, the shift from shortage to surplus in health manpower, and various aspects of hospital economics. This volume examines in detail both the Medicare and Medicaid programs and considers the economic implications of HMOs. The final chapter discusses some of the newer approaches to health care delivery, such as the growth of privatization in the form of alternative birth centers, emergency-care centers, and urgent-care centers and the movement to encourage self-care. Numerous statistical tables help explain complex information.

Stoline, Anne, and Jonathan Weiner. **The New Medical Marketplace.** Baltimore: Johns Hopkins University Press, 1988. 210p. Bibliography. Index. $26.50; $12.95 (paper). ISBN 0-8018-3644-1; 0-8018-3645-X (paper).

Although written for medical professionals, this book is a valuable resource for the lay reader interested in the evolution of health care in the United States and a succinct overview of the current crisis. It is intended as a guide for coping with the many challenges the new health care system offers to medical practice, financing, and ethics. Particularly valuable are the sections that explain the operations of HMOs, PPOs, and the current variety of insurance mechanisms. Costs are considered from the perspective of the health care provider, the payer, and the consumer. Final chapters examine the malpractice crisis and the effect that the need for cost curtailment is having on medical ethics. This volume is an excellent, balanced summary of the myriad factors contributing to the current health care crisis.

Szumski, Bonnie, ed. **The Health Crisis: Opposing Viewpoints.** San Diego: Greenhaven Press, 1989. 285p. Bibliography. Index. $15.95; $7.95 (paper). ISBN 0-89908-438-9; 0-89908-413-3 (paper).

This book is a part of the *Opposing Viewpoints* series published by Greenhaven Press for college-level students and lay readers. This volume presents opposite points of view on the complex issue of the health care crisis, with articles by a variety of authors. The editors encourage the reader to apply critical thinking to the opposite points of view presented. The reader is given exercises that help identify deceptive arguments and distinguish the difference between fact and opinion. Contributing writers consider whether a health care crisis exists, whether private industry makes health care more efficient, and whether the government should provide more health care benefits for the elderly. The book also includes a discussion on the costs of health care and the possible benefits of a holistic life-style.

Turner, Gerald P., and Joseph Mapa, eds. **Humanistic Health Care: Issues for Caregivers.** Ann Arbor, MI: Health Administration Press, 1988. 290p. Bibliography. Index. $30.00. ISBN 0-910701-36-9.

This collection of articles was selected from the vast literature on humanism in health care. The articles focus attention on and sensitize the reader to the importance of providing health care in a supportive and compassionate way. The range and complexity of technological growth, medical progress, changing delivery systems, financial and competitive pressures, and so forth all make it increasingly difficult for care givers to focus on the emotional and empathic needs of patients. Topics covered include the patient's perspective, the care giver, the institution, care of the elderly, humanistic education, and a bioethical context for humanistic health care. This volume addresses many of the criticisms raised by those who complain that the lack of a humanistic approach is one of the significant problems in the current health care system.

Aging

Callahan, Daniel. **Setting Limits: Medical Goals in an Aging Society.** New York: Simon & Schuster, 1987. 256p. Bibliography. Index. $9.95. ISBN 0-671-66831-5.

This book examines the proper goals of medicine in a rapidly aging society where limited medical resources are causing a health care crisis. It is written in easily understandable language by the cofounder and director of the Hastings Center, which is well-known for work on medical ethics. It takes the stance that a disproportionate share of our health care resources is spent on extending the lives of the elderly, with little thought to the quality of those lives. We should shift our attention to relief of suffering and limit care that is merely life extending. An increasingly large proportion of health care and medical research is devoted to the elderly in comparison with benefits for children. This controversial treatise poses a number of difficult ethical questions, such as whether to ration health care among generations and how to find a better way to respond to the inevitability of aging and death in our society. This book won the Pulitzer Prize for nonfiction in 1988.

Kane, Rosalie A., and Robert L. Kane. **Long-Term Care: Principles, Programs, and Policies.** New York: Springer Publishing Company, 1987. 422p. Bibliography. Index. $34.95. ISBN 0-8261-6010-7.

This comprehensive volume presents an overview of current long-term-care systems, reviewing the merits of nursing-home care, adult day care, respite care, and home care. Numerous tables and survey results are cited at length. Some of this material may provide greater detail than is useful for the general reader; however, the concluding chapter summarizing the results of this research provides a wealth of useful information. The book concludes that although much is known about the nature of long-term care and the characteristics of those who receive it, the best ways to deliver it have not yet been determined. The substantial dissatisfaction with the current state of care and an increasing demand for it indicate that more research into this topic is needed.

Nassif, Janet Zhun. **The Home Health Care Solution.** New York: Harper & Row, 1985. 433p. Index. $17.45; $9.95 (paper). ISBN 0-06-015471-3; 0-06-096012-4 (paper).

The rapidly growing home health care industry offers a wide range of services to patients of all ages. It is seen by many as a solid solution to the rising costs of traditional hospital and nursing-home care. This book offers a full definition of what home health care is, plus what it can and cannot offer. It covers how to choose home health care, how to pay for it, and how to obtain special equipment and specialized services such as rehabilitation therapy and hospice care. The concluding chapters are a resource guide to home care that provide checklists and the names of specific organizations nationwide.

Ory, Marcia G., and Kathleen Bond, eds. **Aging and Health Care: Social Science and Policy Perspectives.** London: Routledge, 1989. 265p. Bibliography. Index. $49.95; $19.95 (paper). ISBN 0-415-01716-5; 0-415-01717-3 (paper).

The theme of this book is the need to use a social science perspective as a base for health care policy and practice. It explores the complex relationships among aging people, their health care needs, and the current health care system. Although written in complex social scientific language often unfamiliar to the average reader, it does provide an excellent array of statistics about aging and health care. The epilogue discusses the future challenges in providing health care for an aging population.

Cost Containment

Davis, Karen, Gerard F. Anderson, et al. **Health Care Cost Containment.** Baltimore: Johns Hopkins University Press, 1990. 266p. Bibliography.

Index. $45.00; $18.95 (paper). ISBN 0-8018-3874-6; 0-8018-3875-4 (paper).

Attempts to curb health care costs have been sporadic and largely unsuccessful. This book gives a detailed analysis of cost-containment efforts since the 1950s, including government curbs on Medicare, state cutbacks on Medicaid, and corporate efforts to stem the rising costs of employee benefit plans. All efforts have been fragmented and lack any cohesive guiding policy other than limiting expenses, which leads to a distortion of our overall health policy. This comprehensive volume includes a detailed analysis of the diagnosis-related group (DRG) system, Medicaid, Medicare, corporate cost-containment initiatives, HMOs, and so on. It also covers the impact of cost-containment measures on the poor and on the quality of care. Options for long-range solutions are offered.

Eastaugh, Steven R. **Financing Health Care: Economic Efficiency and Equity.** Dover, MA: Auburn House, 1987. 720p. Bibliography. Index. $49.95; $17.95 (paper). ISBN 0-86569-150-9; 0-86569-161-4 (paper).

This complex volume provides a synthesis of currently available study results on financing health care. It attempts to provide a better understanding of medical economics and financial management literature by examining various cost-containment proposals in the light of currently available research. Topics include managerial concerns among the buyers and sellers of health care, quality and productivity control, medical schools and cost control, cost-effectiveness and cost-benefit measures, and future policy options. Numerous charts and graphs illustrate the text. Although segments of this thorough book are too technical for the average reader, it provides an excellent resource on how financing relates to the health care crisis.

Marsh, Frank H., and Mark Yarborough. **Medicine and Money: A Study of the Role of Beneficence in Health Care Cost Containment.** New York: Greenwood Press, 1990. 171p. Bibliography. Index. $41.55. ISBN 0-313-26357-4.

Health care is increasingly being treated in economic terms, as evidenced by the common usage of such terms as "health care consumer" and "cost containment." This book asks how the medical field can preserve the moral dimensions of beneficence in today's cost-driven environment. It examines the events leading up to the current crisis and the accompanying diminishment of the role of beneficence as the central ethic in the physician-patient relationship, proposing ways to implement beneficence as an effective measure in helping to control escalating costs. Although primarily addressed to physicians and medical students, this volume is of interest to the general reader as well.

McCue, Jack D., ed. **The Medical Cost-Containment Crisis: Fears, Opinions, and Facts.** Ann Arbor, MI: Health Administration Press Perspectives, 1989. 310p. Bibliography. Index. $28.00. ISBN 0-910701-43-1.

Authors representing a wide range of fields contributed essays to this excellent book on containing medical costs. General topics include the relationship between doctor and patient; the viewpoints of business, government, and the medical-industrial complex; a review of the history of cost-containment efforts; and projections for the future. Not all the essays agree with one another, and the emphasis differs, depending on the field of expertise of each author. However, the reader does obtain a balanced overview of medical cost containment. Several of the chapters include up-to-date statistical tables and charts.

McLennan, Kenneth, and Jack A. Meyer, eds. **Care and Cost: Current Issues in Health Policy.** Boulder, CO: Westview Press, 1989. 231p. Bibliography. $24.50. ISBN 0-8133-7609-2.

This collection of essays is part of a study on health care costs funded by the Robert Wood Johnson Foundation. The emphasis is on how market-oriented policies could be used to improve the tradeoffs between cost constraint and greater quality and availability of health care. The book is divided into three main topic areas: catastrophic and long-term care, practitioner issues, and workplace issues. The introductory chapter by the editors provides an excellent overview of trends in the health care field, while Chapter 6 offers a careful analysis of the costs of medical malpractice suits.

Schramm, Carl J., ed. **Health Care and Its Costs.** New York: W.W. Norton and Company, 1987. 301p. Index. $18.95; $7.95 (paper). ISBN 0-393-02437-7; 0-393-95671-7 (paper).

This collection of essays related to health care costs examines possible answers to the question of how to resolve the United States' health care crisis. Contributing authors include representatives from such fields as education, medicine, insurance, and hospital and finance management. All were participants in the 1986 American Assembly, which has held nonpartisan national meetings each year since 1950 to discuss matters of vital public interest. The book includes an assessment of public opinion and health care costs, insurance, the changing role of the physician, and several chapters on the relationship of the aging population to health care costs. Chapter 9 is the final report of the 1986 American Assembly, which includes 12 recommendations for national action.

Ethics

Blank, Robert H. **Life, Death, and Public Policy.** DeKalb, IL: Northern Illinois University Press, 1988. 177p. Bibliography. Index. $22.50; $8.50 (paper). ISBN 0-87580-142-0; 0-87580-540-X (paper).

This book places biomedical issues in a policy context. Of particular interest are the cultural themes that affect the politics of biomedicine. These themes, which enjoy near-consensual support, include a heavy emphasis on the notion of rights, an obsession with the prolongation of life, and a predisposition toward progress through technological means. Another factor that affects the diverse and complex biomedical system is the third-party reimbursement system, which insulates much of the public from the real costs of meeting its high expectations. Because of the inability of other branches of government to address the issues raised by biomedical innovations, the courts currently play a central role in policymaking. The power of the media and interest groups in influencing public policy is also discussed. This excellent volume concludes that the United States can no longer afford to embrace technology for its own sake. Long-term implications of each application must be assessed before it is used.

Blank, Robert H. **Rationing Medicine.** New York: Columbia University Press, 1988. 290p. Bibliography. Index. $14.50. ISBN 0-231-06536-1.

Medical policymakers must make decisions in the near future to avert impending disaster. Four aspects of health care are discussed, including organ transplantation, treatment of seriously ill newborns, reproductive technologies, and fetal health. The United States must moderate public expectations of biomedical technologies and emphasize preventive health care. Today's high-cost, high-technology curative and rescue efforts cannot continue at the same rapid pace. The United States must shift to a health care model based on individual responsibility and life-style choices. Too many of the country's resources are spent on illnesses linked to smoking, alcohol and drug use, poor diet, and inadequate exercise. An effective rationing policy must emphasize such choices. Despite the problems inherent in moving toward the rationing of medicine, rationing will become more prevalent and more overt.

Brody, Baruch A. **Life and Death Decision Making.** New York: Oxford University Press, 1988. 250p. Index. $29.95. ISBN 0-19-505007-X.

This book examines the practical application of moral theory in clinical decision making. Using 40 composite cases based on actual clinical experience, it takes a careful look at key moral problems raised by modern medicine. An attempt is made to synthesize traditional moral theories, such as the consequences of actions, rights, respect for persons, virtues, cost-effectiveness, and justice. Each case study gives the facts of the case, raises ethical questions, and concludes with a theoretical analysis. Although the language in this book is complex for the average reader, the use of case studies keeps this volume from being too theoretical. The notes at the end of each chapter list ample up-to-date resources for the reader interested in pursuing this complex topic further.

Callahan, Daniel. **What Kind of Life: The Limits of Medical Progress.** New York: Simon & Schuster, 1990. 318p. Bibliography. Index. $19.95. ISBN 0-671-67096-4.

This philosophical approach is a plea for a switch from an individual to a societal perspective in dealing with health care. Our society incorrectly believes that health equals human happiness. We must admit that death and disease are inevitable and find a way to prioritize communal needs over individual ones. Doctors' offices will always be full, no matter how much progress is made. There will always be pain, death, and suffering, and there will always be a medical frontier. We need to devise a fuller way of life that values more than its length. Our country must provide basic health care for all, but set limits on individual requirements for highly advanced medical therapy. The final chapter discusses the controversial topic of euthanasia.

Garrett, Thomas M. **Health Care Ethics: Principles and Problems.** Englewood Cliffs, NJ: Prentice Hall, 1989. 271p. Bibliography. Index. $24.60. ISBN 0-13-385063-3.

This concise textbook defines principles of health care ethics in the first section and discusses specific ethical problems in the second section. It includes an excellent, understandable definition of the major theories of ethics. Step by step, the reader is carefully taken through a lot of theoretical material that is kept brief and comprehensible. Cases for analysis are presented at the end of each chapter. The final chapters cover the ethical problems of death and dying, abortion, new methods of reproduction, and the ethics of transplants, testing, and biomedical research.

Humphrey, Derek, and Ann Wickett. **The Right To Die: Understanding Euthanasia.** New York: Harper & Row, 1986. 372p. Bibliography. Index. $18.45. ISBN 0-06-015578-7.

This book on a person's right to end his or her own life starts with an extensive historical section on attitudes toward death. With the advent of new technologies, the interest in euthanasia has increased. Membership in and support for euthanasia advocacy groups are growing steadily. The book discusses the "mixed blessing" aspects of high technology in prolonging life, the legal aspects of mercy killing, and attempts to define death itself. The topic of euthanasia is covered objectively, with numerous case histories pointing out ethical dilemmas. The appendixes include films dealing with dying and organizations dealing with death.

Hyde, Margaret O., and Elizabeth H. Forsyth. **Medical Dilemmas.** New York: G. P. Putnam's Sons, 1990. 112p. Index. $14.95. ISBN 0-399-21902-1.

Along with the advances of modern medical technology have come medical dilemmas. This book examines such ethical questions as who should receive organ transplants, how long expensive and painful treatment should be continued for brain-damaged babies, and who has the right to decide to discontinue life-support systems. Of particular interest are chapters on the ethics of animal research and AIDS, two topics not covered in older books on medical ethics. Written in easily understood language, the book introduces ethical questions but leaves it up to readers to make up their own minds. The book includes a list of suggested readings for further research.

Kilner, John F. **Who Lives? Who Dies? Ethical Criteria in Patient Selection.** New Haven, CT: Yale University Press, 1990. 359p. Bibliography. Index. $29.95. ISBN 0-300-04680-4.

More lives can be saved than ever before because of recent breakthroughs in medical science. However, with too few financial and other resources to provide these technological advances to everyone, how can it be decided who receives medical treatment? This book examines the pros and cons of 16 patient-selection criteria, such as deciding which patients will be of greatest value to society if saved, whether to favor young patients over elderly ones, and who can medically benefit most from the procedure. Case histories help make the ethical discussions understandable for the lay reader. In addition to being well-written, this book is valuable for its extensive notes and bibliography.

McKenzie, Nancy F. **The Crisis in Health Care: Ethical Issues.** New York: Penguin Books, 1990. 640p. $12.95. ISBN 0-452-01028-4.

This collection of essays is about the ethics of *care,* not cure, with a focus on the medically unserved, such as children, the homeless, the uninsured, and others that the health care system fails. Today some 37 million Americans are without any form of public or private health insurance, which leaves them virtually without medical care. This grim fact, coupled with the growing AIDS and drug epidemics, has converted our priorities as human beings into literal questions of life and death.

The essays in this provocative book ask uncomfortable questions, such as where physicians get organ transplants and who gets them. It explores fetal research, life supports for the hopelessly ill, HMOs, and the current crisis in medical education. Contributing writers include leading thinkers and clinical practitioners in the health care field.

Menzel, Paul T. **Strong Medicine: The Ethical Rationing of Health Care.** New York: Oxford University Press, 1990. 234p. Bibliography. Index. $25.95. ISBN 0-19-505710-4.

The current health care crisis pits the demand for efficiency against the needs of the individual patient. As health care costs continue to soar, we must find a better ethical framework for making rational decisions. In considerable detail, this book poses many intriguing ethical questions. Topics discussed in readily understandable language include a patient's consent to risk, pricing of life, measuring quality of life, equality of care, and organ transplants. Of particular interest are chapters on the effects of the nonprofit competitive environment on health care and the cost of malpractice litigation. The book concludes with a thought-provoking chapter on the individual's "duty to die cheaply."

Scully, Thomas, and Celia Scully. **Playing God.** New York: Simon & Schuster, 1987. 431p. Bibliography. Index. $19.95. ISBN 0-671-60144-X.

This is a practical, comprehensive guide for patients and families faced with difficult health care questions. Written in a personal, how-to-do-it style, the book explains in everyday language such concepts as patients' rights and informed consent. Topics range from living wills to transplanting human organs to the bioethics of new techniques such as *in vitro* fertilization. Chapter 10 details how to get action in the case of malpractice or billing fraud. The extensive appendix includes samples of patients' bills of rights, a living will, and the addresses of national and regional centers for medical ethics.

Suzuki, David, and Peter Knudtson. **Genethics: The Clash between the New Genetics and Human Values.** Cambridge, MA: Harvard University Press, 1989. 384p. Bibliography. Index. $25.00. ISBN 0-674-34565-7.

The first five chapters of this technical volume explain what genes are and how they work. Numerous illustrations help explain this complex material. The remainder of the book presents case studies that illustrate the ethical issues involved in the rapidly changing field of genetics. They cover such topics as genetic screening, somatic-cell versus germ-cell strategies of gene therapy, various possible classes of biological warfare, and current plans to sequence the human genome. If the opening chapters are too technical, readers interested in the ethical aspects of genetic engineering can skip them and focus on

Chapters 6 through 13. The final chapter proposes ten ethical principles that should serve as moral guidelines for genetic responsibility.

Hospitals and HMOs

Altman, Stuart H., et al. **Competition and Compassion.** Ann Arbor, MI: Health Administration Press, 1989. 221p. Index. $30.00. ISBN 0-910701-37-7.

Although urban public hospitals represent only a small minority of the nonfederal public hospitals in the United States, they serve many patients who have no other source of health care, such as Medicaid enrollees and uninsured indigents. These hospitals provide a disproportionately high volume of ambulatory services, burn units, alcoholism treatment programs, neonatal intensive-care units, and psychiatric emergency units and are frequently the site of care for victims of crime and life-threatening trauma. Traditionally underfunded, these hospitals are suffering under the burden of new problems. Cutbacks in Medicaid eligibility and severe unemployment have led to growing numbers of uninsured urban residents. In addition, the DRG system leads private hospitals to transfer unprofitable long-term Medicare patients to public hospitals, further increasing their costs. This comprehensive volume assesses the performance of public hospitals, considering case histories of four major hospitals, and concludes with general principles for improving the performance at urban public hospitals.

Bloom, Jill. **HMOs: What They Are, How They Work, and Which One Is Best for You.** Tucson, AZ: The Body Press, 1987. 277p. Index. $19.95; $9.95 (paper). ISBN 0-89586-645-5; 0-89586-557-2 (paper).

This consumer's guide examines the five major types of HMOs and covers both sides of the controversy surrounding their existence. It explains how each type of HMO functions and how to determine which type might work for individual consumers. It also takes a look into the future of health care and examines what directions HMOs might take. The final section is an extensive resource guide that includes a national HMO directory arranged by state. Although directed at consumers, this book is an excellent resource for anyone trying to understand in detail what an HMO is and how it works.

Frech, H. E. **Health Care in America: Political Economy of Hospitals and Health Insurance.** San Francisco: Pacific Research Institute for Public Policy, 1988. 401p. Bibliography. Index. $34.95. ISBN 0-936488-18-2.

This book of essays written by economists analyzes health care in the United States from an economic point of view. The first chapter gives an overview of health care, while the following chapters consider more specialized topics such as the hospital industry, government involvement in health care, and private health insurance. Although the book is fairly technical, the language is comprehensible to the lay reader. As pointed out in the introduction, current trends in health care are encouraging the consideration of health care from an economic perspective. Recent attempts to curtail costs, increased marketing and competition in the health care sector, and the growth of for-profit organizations all point to a rising interest in the economics of health care.

Seay, J. David, and Bruce C. Vladeck, eds. **In Sickness and Health: The Mission of Voluntary Health Care Institutions.** New York: McGraw-Hill, 1988. 232p. $32.95. ISBN 0-07-067532-5.

Throughout U.S. history, most general hospitals, institutional outpatient services, and formal home care have been provided by nonprofit, nongovernmental organizations. However, the role of nonprofit providers of health care is increasingly being attacked. They are criticized for their tax-exempt status, especially as they have diversified into a number of enterprises that make it hard to differentiate them from proprietary institutions. Through a series of essays by different authors, this book examines whether there is a unique role for voluntary health care institutions. The conclusion predicts that as general hospital care loses its lucrative appeal and returns to a "nonmarket" enterprise, the voluntary hospital will again dominate the U.S. health care system.

Stevens, Mary. **In Sickness and in Wealth: American Hospitals in the Twentieth Century.** New York: Basic Books, Inc., 1989. 432p. Bibliography. Index. $24.95. ISBN 0-465-03223-0.

This history of U.S. hospitals in the twentieth century places these vital institutions in a moral, social, and political context. As a native of England, the author has a perspective that enhances this review of the U.S. hospital system. Voluntary, nonprofit hospitals have been expansionary, income-maximizing institutions throughout the twentieth century. However, they have simultaneously carried social significance as a symbol of American hopes and ideals. Added to this traditional mix of hospital roles have been incentives by the federal government to encourage hospitals to operate as for-profit, competitive businesses. Today this varied system is in a state of crisis as it struggles with unresolved conflicts and future directions. Hospitals have provided the most advanced medical care for the acutely ill and curable patients, but the question remains whether they fill the increasingly unmet needs of the chronically ill and the socially disadvantaged.

Weeks, Lewis E., and Howard J. Berman. **Shapers of American Health Care Policy.** Ann Arbor, MI: Health Administration Press, 1985. 345p. Bibliography. Index. $29.00. ISBN 0-910701-09-1.

Based on oral histories, this book provides excellent background material on the evolution of hospital care in the United States. A chronology of significant events in hospital history is given from the turn of the century through the establishment of Medicare in 1965. It focuses on the three major events that provided the foundation for the current hospital operating environment: the work of the Committee on the Costs of Medical Care, the Hospital Survey and Construction Act (Hill-Burton), and Medicare/Medicaid legislation. The history of Blue Cross and the American Hospital Association are also covered. Personal reminiscences about major events in health care history include those by Wilbur Cohen, Wilbur Mills, Nelson Cruikshank, Walter McNerney, Daniel Pettengill, Kenneth Williamson, John Mannix, and Maurice Norby. The final chapter contains a summary of five decades of change and a projection for the future.

Medical Malpractice

Baily, Mary Ann, and Warren I. Cikins, eds. **The Effects of Litigation on Health Care Costs.** Washington, DC: The Brookings Institution, 1985. 85p. $9.85. ISBN 0-8157-0757-6.

This volume is one of a series of *Brookings Dialogues on Public Policy,* and is a collection of papers presented at a conference entitled "The Effects of Litigation on Health Care Costs." Presenters were drawn from both the health care and the legal communities, and they achieved a consensus that litigation is a key contributor to the rising cost of health care. Litigation itself is expensive, but fear of litigation leads doctors to practice "defensive medicine" and order possibly unnecessary tests and procedures to protect themselves against suits. The fear of litigation may also make doctors and hospitals reluctant to eliminate care that is of little benefit relative to cost. The essays conclude that although malpractice litigation is central to the cost problem, little is known about the precise costs and benefits of the tort liability system as it affects health care. Reform is necessary, but no consensus exists on what solutions are appropriate.

Charles, Sara C., and Eugene Kennedy. **Defendant: A Psychiatrist on Trial for Medical Malpractice.** New York: The Free Press, 1985. 230p. Index. $17.95; $7.95 (paper). ISBN 0-02-905910-0; 0-394-74663-5 (paper).

This is the true story of the dramatic trial of a psychiatrist involved in malpractice litigation. The story is twofold: the one, a gripping courtroom drama; the other, a national health care crisis. The book reveals the enormous professional and personal burdens these suits place on physicians and their effect on our health care system and on the patients themselves. Fear of lawsuits has not only led doctors to the expensive and unnecessary practice of defensive medicine, but it has also brought about the diminished availability of medical services. (The number of practicing obstetrician-gynecologists, for example, is down by 10 percent nationwide.) Malpractice suits are driving up the price of medicine as patients are asked to compensate for their physicians' rising insurance premiums. The book concludes with a plea for public outcry to demand solutions to the crisis.

Edwards, Frank J. **Medical Malpractice: Solving the Crisis.** New York: Henry Holt and Company, 1989. 182p. Bibliography. $22.50. ISBN 0-8050-0428-9.

Written by a physician, this book addresses the medical malpractice crisis in the United States. Suing physicians has become an industry. Out of every 100 physicians practicing in 1989, eight to ten could expect to be named in a lawsuit. The statistics are even higher for certain specialties. As a result, doctors are paying extremely high insurance premiums and practicing defensive medicine by ordering extensive tests. Some of them are even quitting the profession. The medical malpractice crisis is a major contributor to rising health care costs. Lawyers, insurance companies, and physicians themselves are often cited as the culprits in the crisis. Although not claiming to have all of the answers, the author suggests that the introduction of complaint boards and some form of arbitration process would be a step in the right direction.

King, Joseph H., Jr. **The Law of Medical Malpractice in a Nutshell.** St. Paul, MN: West Publishing Company, 1986. 342p. Index. $10.95. ISBN 0-314-98200-0.

Despite a decade of attempts by the states to stem the rising tide of malpractice litigation through law reform, the number and size of claims continue to grow. Since the constitutionality of much reform legislation has been challenged, it remains unclear whether this is a legislative realm or whether it remains in the traditional domain of the judiciary. In layperson's language, the book offers a historical perspective on this complex field and a succinct definition of terms. Major categories of malpractice are discussed, concluding with current perspectives and future prospects in the field. No simple solutions are offered, but the book states that something must be done to end the unpredictability and virtually limitless liability exposure of health care professionals, which is undermining the physician-patient relationship and consuming such a high share of the nation's resources.

Lander, Louise. **Defective Medicine: Risk, Anger, and the Malpractice Crisis.** New York: Farrar, Straus and Giroux, 1978. 242p. Bibliography. Index. $10.00. ISBN 0-374-13627-0.

This book is older than most listings in this chapter, but it is included because of the excellent section explaining how the insurance industry works (see Chapters 8, 9, and 10). It provides a history and a balanced overview of the medical malpractice crisis. In the author's opinion, physicians, lawyers, and the insurance industry are not the culprits; the crux of the problem lies in the increasing depersonalization of medical care. As medicine has become more and more institutionalized, technology oriented, and specialized, the patient has been reduced to a commodity. The increased use of lawsuits is a symptom of increased patient frustration and dissatisfaction. Medical practice needs to be demystified and the human reality of sickness taken into account.

Robertson, William O. **Medical Malpractice: A Preventive Approach.** Seattle: University of Washington Press, 1985. 212p. Bibliography. Index. $20.00. ISBN 0-205-96162-7.

Over 90 percent of all the malpractice suits ever filed in the United States have been filed in the last two decades. At the present time, one out of every ten physicians in this country is involved in an alleged incident of malpractice. This book discusses the causes and cures for the burgeoning lawsuits, large awards, and rapidly escalating insurance premiums causing the malpractice crisis. The points of view of both patients and health professionals are considered. The appendix lists 30 "risk management review units," case histories that highlight potential problem areas and their most effective solutions. Although written for health professionals, this easy-to-read volume is of interest to the general reader as well.

Sociology of Medicine

Anderson, Odin W. **Health Services in the United States: A Growth Enterprise Since 1875.** Ann Arbor, MI: Health Administration Press, 1985. 293p. Index. $29.00. ISBN 0-910701-02-4.

This volume provides an excellent historical survey of the development of health services from a sociological and political perspective. Three periods of development are identified: the emergence of the basic services of the current system (1875–1930), the era of the third-party payment system (1930–1965), and the era of management and control (1965 to the present). The book defines the common elements of a health care system and illustrates the need to examine the system in a larger social and political context. It also emphasizes the importance of the political process in allocating health resources. Although written in an academic style, this book is a good resource for a historical overview of the evolution of modern health care in the United States.

Ginzberg, Eli, ed. **Medicine and Society: Clinical Decisions and Societal Values.** Boulder, CO: Westview Press, 1987. 153p. Index. $26.50. ISBN 0-8133-0574-8.

This collection of essays by prominent figures in the health care field is drawn from papers presented at the Cornell University Medical College Third Conference on Health Policy in 1987. Its theme is the translation of societal values into health care objectives and the forming of mechanisms to guide the process of making clinical decisions. The authors agree that everyone should have access to essential health care and that care should be delivered efficiently in a cost-effective manner. However, defining "essential health care" and what is "cost-effective" is a matter of some debate. Although several of the essays are related to the clinical treatment of cardiovascular diseases, organ transplants, and other specific treatments, other essays are of interest to the general reader. In "A Twentieth Century Retrospective," Robert H. Ebert provides an informative overview of health care in this century, and "Themes and Policies" by Eli Ginzberg offers an interpretive review of all the essays.

Mechanic, David. **From Advocacy to Allocation.** New York: The Free Press, 1986. 238p. Bibliography. Index. $24.95; $12.95 (paper). ISBN 0-02-920830-0; 0-02-920860-2 (paper).

The U.S. health care system is in the throes of a scientific, philosophical, and economic revolution. A prominent medical sociologist examines the issues involved in this revolution, touching on such topics as medical care and social policy, approaches to controlling costs, and rationing strategies. Also discussed with considerable insight are changes in the health professions whereby doctors and hospitals have moved from their traditional role of *advocating* to *allocating* health care resources. Of particular value to the general reader is the introduction, which gives an overview of the U.S. health care system. The book concludes with a discussion of the ethical dilemmas inherent in the allocation of health care services.

Mechanic, David. **Painful Choices: Research and Essays on Health Care.** New Brunswick, NJ: Transaction Publishers, 1989. 248p. Bibliographies. $34.95. ISBN 0-88738-258-4.

How wisely society makes the painful choices in the allocation of health care resources will determine the quality and character of health care for years to come. This book examines the existing dilemmas and explores conceptual approaches to health care. The key challenge will be to respond to the growing numbers of the uninsured, the frail elderly, and patients with serious mental illnesses and other chronic disabilities. Health services must be shaped to enhance function and quality of life, not simply to respond to technological imperatives. Although this book provides an excellent framework for policy analysis, it will be difficult reading for those unfamiliar with sociological concepts and language.

Stein, Howard F. **American Medicine as Culture.** Boulder, CO: Westview Press, 1990. 281p. Bibliography. Index. $25.95. ISBN 0-8133-0737-6.

This study of U.S. medicine as a cultural system identifies the subtle patterns and themes that underlie this country's diverse medical system. It is addressed to behavioral scientists, health professionals, teachers, and the lay public. The U.S. medical system is obsessed with activity and procedural prowess, which is leading to an increasing emphasis on medical care as a commodity. This profound shift in values results in a diminishing of compassion as cost containment becomes tantamount. Intriguing topics are discussed, such as the true meaning of the wellness movement. Rather than a trend toward better health, this movement is portrayed as an anti-intellectual attitude that substitutes action for insight. It leads to social Darwinism, praising the survival of the fittest and allowing the needs of the chronically ill, the elderly, and other "unfit" segments of the population to be overlooked. Especially thought-provoking is the final chapter on how personal and cultural attitudes affect an individual physician's approach to the practice of medicine.

Trends in Health Care

Amara, Roy. **Looking Ahead at American Health Care.** Washington, DC: McGraw-Hill, 1988. 199p. $95.00. ISBN 0-07-001384-5.

This report by the Institute for the Future, of Menlo Park, California, singles out the trends most likely to change health care. It describes two different scenarios that are most likely to emerge and identifies the key choices that will face us by the year 2000. The report's goal is to provide long-term planning assistance to health professional groups, private foundations, public- and private-sector decision makers, and professional associations. Key environmental forces creating change in the health care system are identified. These include aging, more sophisticated consumers, pressures from payers, increasing technology, a rise in the number of doctors, and the involvement of the government as a purchaser and regulator of health care. Of particular interest are the many tables projecting two different scenarios for health care through the year 2000.

Butler, Stuart M., and Edmund F. Haislmaier, eds. **A National Health System for America.** Washington, DC: The Heritage Foundation, 1989. 127p. $8.00. ISBN 0-89195-049-4.

The U.S. health care system is on the critical list and needs intensive care. Although many policymakers propose that the solution to this crisis is a national system based on the European or the Canadian model, those systems have many serious shortcomings. A national system is not the only alternative, and this small but comprehensive volume offers alternative proposals for reform. The book begins with an excellent survey of how today's basic health care system evolved not in response to the needs of consumers, but according to the marketing and professional objectives of the suppliers of health care. Such a system inevitably led to rising costs, which the book maintains can be corrected by turning the present quasi-market health care system into a true market system. A succinct comparison of the health care systems in other countries is provided.

Coile, Russell C., Jr. **The New Medicine: Reshaping Medical Practice and Health Care Management.** Rockville, MD: Aspen Publishers, Inc., 1990. 395p. Bibliography. Index. $39.95. ISBN 0-8342-0103-8.

This book highlights trends and future directions of the changing health care environment. Although aimed at physicians and hospitals, with strategic implications for each group listed at the end of every chapter, the book is also valuable for the general reader. It features abundant current statistics as well as thought-provoking suggestions for the future. Ten trends in health care are discussed: declining reimbursement and expanding revenues, inpatient renaissance, ambulatory hospitals, specialty niches, managed care, aging population, regional and national hospital networks, service-oriented management, service management, and outcome management. The author claims that although cost reimbursement characterized health care through 1983, and 1983 through 1989 was an era of competition, managed care will dominate the end of the twentieth century and beyond. Chapter 21 proposes four alternative scenarios for the future of medicine in the year 2000.

Journals and Periodicals

In a book of this size, an attempt to list all of the journals and periodicals that cover topics related to the U.S. health care crisis is bound to end in frustration. It is an extremely complex topic and one that is covered in periodicals intended for the general public as well as those for a more specialized readership. Many of the titles included in the following list are drawn from newsletters published by a wide range of organizations involved in the health care field. Most represent a slightly different point of view, relative to their positions in the health care industry; however, some of the journals listed present a broader overview of the topic.

AARP Bulletin
Newsletter of the American Association of Retired Persons (AARP)
3200 East Carson Street
Lakewood, CA 90712
(202) 872-4700
Monthly, except August. Annual AARP dues are $5, which includes 85 cents for annual subscription.

AARP is a nonprofit, nonpartisan organization with 32 million members aged 50 and over. The bulletin provides recent news from the Executive Branch, Congress, courts, regulatory agencies, and state legislatures. It also reports on trends that have a bearing on the lives of older citizens.

Advances
The Robert Wood Johnson Foundation
Communications Office
P.O. Box 2316
Princeton, NJ 08543-2316
(609) 452-8701
Quarterly. Free. Call to receive a copy or to be placed on regular mailing list.

The Robert Wood Johnson Foundation is a national philanthropy that has given over a billion dollars in grant funds since it began in 1972. Its mission is the improvement of medical care in the United States. *Advances* announces the recipients of grants, reports on the results of studies funded by the foundation, summarizes recently published research by grantees, and generally provides an update on the activities of the foundation.

The Aging Connection
American Society on Aging
833 Market Street, Suite 516
San Francisco, CA 94103
(415) 882-2910
Bimonthly. Members' subscription price of $7.50 included in annual dues; nonmembers $25.

This newspaper provides a forum for discussion of significant current issues in aging. It covers innovative ideas in practice, research, and new products and designs for enhanced living. Legislative news and aging-related events are also covered.

AHA News

American Hospital Publishing, Inc.
211 East Chicago Avenue, Suite 700
Chicago, IL 60611
(312) 440-6800
Fifty times a year. Annual subscription price for members is $45; nonmembers $100.

This eight-page newspaper for health care executives contains late-breaking news from Washington, D.C., and around the country. Contents include news and policy information from the American Hospital Association (AHA); timely legislative, regulatory, and court activities; personal viewpoints from health care leaders; and other topics of interest.

AMCRA Newsletter

American Managed Care and Review Association
1227 Twenty-fifth Street, NW, Suite 610
Washington, DC 20037
(202) 728-0506
Ten times a year. Provided to members and available by subscription for $120.

AMCRA is the professional association representing the managed-care industry. It includes 400 health care organizations such as HMOs, PPOs, and physicians. This newsletter provides information on legislation, court decisions, and other news items of interest to group health care organizations.

American Medical News

American Medical Association
535 North Dearborn Street
Chicago, IL 60610
(312) 645-5000
Forty-eight times a year. Annual subscription is $50; single copy $2.

This newsletter is of greater interest to the general reader than *JAMA* (see below). It covers significant legislation, court decisions, and policy decisions that affect the medical profession. *American Medical News* provides a valuable insight into the physician's point of view about the health care crisis.

American Nurse
American Nurses Association
2420 Pershing Road
Kansas City, MO 64108
(816) 474-5720
Ten times a year. Annual subscription $20; free to members.

This newspaper covers health care issues of interest to professional nurses, such as the future of public health nursing, liability insurance, and the nursing shortage.

American Pharmacy
American Pharmaceutical Association
2215 Constitution Avenue, NW
Washington, DC 20037
(202) 628-4410
Monthly. Annual subscription $45; free to members.

Although many of the topics covered in this journal are of interest only to professional pharmacists, it does include information of value to the general reader, such as a regular feature on legislation and regulation and articles on policy issues related to the health care crisis.

Business & Health
American Health Consultants, in consultation with the Washington Business Group on Health
P.O. Box 2082
Marion, OH 43306
(800) 833-0197
Monthly. Annual subscription $85; single copy $10.

A variety of health care issues of interest to major employers are covered in each issue. Topics run the gamut from wellness programs to how to measure the performance of hospitals. Many articles are of interest to the general reader as well as to employers that provide health care benefits.

Caring
National Association for Home Care
519 C Street, NE
Washington, DC 20002
(202) 547-7424
Monthly. Annual subscription $45; free to members.

This magazine covers topics of interest to professionals in the home health care industry. Typical topics include case management, community-based care, HMOs, visiting nurse services, and reimbursement practices. Although articles are written for professionals, the reader concerned with home health care as an alternative to expensive hospital care may find them of interest.

Generations
833 Market Street, Room 516
San Francisco, CA 94103
(415) 543-2617
Quarterly. Annual subscription $30; single copy $9.

This journal is published by the American Society on Aging to bring together the most useful and current knowledge about specific topics in the field of aging, such as the financing of long-term care. The emphasis is on practice, research, and policy.

Hastings Center Report
255 Elm Road
Briarcliff Manor, NY 10510
(914) 762-8500
Bimonthly. Annual subscription included in membership: $42 for individuals; $35 for full-time students.

This is the official publication of the Hastings Center, which carries out research on timely and crucial subjects, including ethical issues related to health care. The report approaches ethical problems from an interdisciplinary perspective to challenge both the general and the professional reader.

Health Affairs
Project HOPE
Millwood, VA 22646
(703) 837-2100
Quarterly. $35 a year.

This is an excellent resource for articles with an overview of current health care issues. It tracks national health care spending trends in the "DataWatch" section. This journal is indexed in ABI/INFORM, CINAHL, and MEDLINE.

Health Care Financing Review
Superintendent of Documents
U.S. Government Printing Office
Washington, DC 20402
(202) 275-2051
Quarterly. $13 a year; single issue $6.50.

This journal includes statistical reports, research, articles, special reports, health care financing trends, health care indicators, legislative updates, grants and contracts, and news briefs. It is a valuable resource for tracking up-to-date statistics, trends, and resources for further information.

Health Letter
Public Citizen Health Research Group
Circulation Department
2000 P Street, NW
Washington, DC 20036
(202) 872-0320
Monthly. $18 a year; single issue $1.50.

This journal by the Health Research Group of Ralph Nader's Public Citizen organization provides timely and useful information for the health-conscious consumer. Typical topics include choosing safe hospitals and affordable medical care, avoiding carcinogen-contaminated foods, accessing medical records, and saving money by purchasing generic drugs.

Health Services Research
Foundation of the American College of Healthcare Executives
1951 Cornell Avenue
Melrose Park, IL 60160
(312) 943-0544, ext. 3001
Bimonthly. $45 a year; single issue $10.

This journal seeks to facilitate communication among health services researchers, policymakers, and practitioners. The statistics in some articles are very complex, but this journal is a good source of up-to-date statistical information.

Health Values/Health Behavior, Education, and Promotion
PNG Publications
P.O. Box 4593
Star City, WV 26504-4593
Six issues a year. $55 a year; single issue $12.

The purpose of this journal is to improve the health status of individuals, families, and communities by providing a better understanding of health behavior, education, and promotion. It explores the relationships among personal behavior, social structure, and health.

Healthcare Forum Journal
The Healthcare Forum
830 Market Street
San Francisco, CA 94102
(415) 421-8810
Bimonthly. $35 a year; single issue $6.50.

Each issue of this journal focuses on a central theme in health care management, viewing it from a variety of perspectives. Representative topics include market-driven communications strategies, visionary health care leadership, planning for ambulatory care, and physician leadership. Written largely for administrators of health care systems, this magazine does include articles with an overview of health policy.

HMO Magazine
Circulation Department
1129 Twentieth Street, NW
Washington, DC 20036
Bimonthly. Annual subscription $75; single issue $13.

This magazine covers a broad range of issues of concern to HMO executives and managers, including employer relationships, business trends, pharmacy and mental health benefits, claims administration, utilization management, and news of legislative and regulatory changes affecting the HMO industry.

Homecare
National Association for Home Care
519 C Street, NE
Washington, DC 20002
(202) 547-7424
Monthly. Annual subscription $18; free to members.

This publication reaches the home care and hospice industry with timely news about legislation, policy changes, and other events affecting the home health care industry.

Hospitals
American Hospital Publishing, Inc.
211 East Chicago Avenue
Chicago, IL 60611
(800) 621-6902
Twice monthly. $50 a year.

This magazine for health care executives reflects the highly diversified nature of today's health care delivery system. Cover stories address specific topics in depth, such as the nationwide revolution in outpatient care, while other shorter articles cover trends in the hospital industry.

InterStudy Edge
Center for Managed Care Research
P.O. Box 458
Excelsior, MN 55331-0458
(612) 474-1176
Quarterly. $226 a year; single issue $5.

This quarterly report covers the growth of HMOs and other managed-care health systems. Two of the four annual issues list every HMO in the country and provide statistics about enrollment, model type, age of plan, federal qualification status, and profit status. Other issues cover such topics as cost containment, trends, insurance, and employer purchasing strategies.

JAMA
The Journal of the American Medical Association
535 North Dearborn Street
Chicago, IL 60610
(312) 645-5000
Four issues a month. Members $20 a year; nonmembers $69.

With over 297,000 members, the American Medical Association is the largest organization of physicians in the United States. Its purpose is to preserve the art and science of medicine and to protect the public health. The organization's official journal includes numerous technical articles on specific aspects of medicine that would be unintelligible to the average reader. However, most issues also include articles providing an overview of developments in the health care field, discussions of policy, ethical matters, and so on.

Modern Maturity
American Association of Retired Persons (AARP)
3200 East Carson Street
Lakewood, CA 90712
Monthly. $240 annual subscription includes $5 annual AARP membership dues.

This journal of the AARP covers a broad spectrum of topics of interest to older Americans, including health care.

The Nation's Health
American Public Health Association
1015 Fifteenth Street, NW
Washington, DC 20005
(202) 789-5636
Eleven times a year. $12 a year; single issue $2.

This newspaper reports on current and proposed legislation, policy issues, and news of action within the federal agencies and Congress. Features provide forums for discussions on current health issues, planning and development, regulatory actions, and related topics.

Networks
National Council on the Aging, Inc. (NCOA)
600 Maryland Avenue, SW
West Wing 100
Washington, DC 20024
(202) 479-6985
Bimonthly. Included with NCOA membership.

This newsletter highlights specific activities of NCOA, reports legislative and regulatory activity and judicial decisions affecting older persons, and explores significant developments in the field of aging.

New England Journal of Medicine
10 Shattuck Street
Boston, MA 02115-6094
Weekly. $79 a year.

This well-known, prestigious journal is often quoted in the press as a source of medical news. Although many articles are highly technical and of interest only to medical professionals, special articles and editorials often provide an overview of health care and address various aspects of the health care crisis.

Perspective on Aging
National Council on the Aging, Inc. (NCOA)
600 Maryland Avenue, SW
West Wing 100
Washington, DC 20024
(202) 479-6985
Bimonthly. Included with NCOA membership; $3.50 single copy.

This is the official publication of the National Council on the Aging (NCOA), which is the nation's leading organization of professionals providing services to older persons. The journal provides an overview of new ideas in program development, policy, and research.

PPO Perspectives
American Association of Preferred Provider Organizations (AAPPO)
111 East Wacker Drive, Suite 600
Chicago, IL 60601
(312) 644-6610, ext. 3270
Bimonthly. Included with AAPPO membership; $125 annually for nonmembers.

This newsletter features conferences, legislative columns, membership news, and regional news. The legislative news would be of the most interest to general readers.

Priorities
American Council on Science and Health
1995 Broadway, 16th Floor
New York, NY 10023-5860
(212) 362-7044
Quarterly. $50.

This magazine is published by the American Council on Science and Health, Inc., a nonprofit consumer education association promoting scientifically balanced evaluations of nutrition, chemicals, life-style factors, the environment, and human health. The content ranges from articles on public health policy and ethics to analyses of specific questions about health, such as liposuction, prenatal testing, and alar in apples.

Public Health Reports
Journal of the U.S. Public Health Service
Office of the Assistant Secretary for Health, Room 725-H
Hubert Humphrey Building
200 Independence Avenue, SW
Washington, DC 20201
(301) 443-0762
Bimonthly. $9 a year; single issue $4.75.

The journal of the U.S. Public Health Service contains numerous specific articles on such topics as the status of community water fluoridation in the United States and trends in AIDS incidence. However, some issues address general topics relevant to the health care crisis, such as the influence of the media in health communication, improving the health of minorities, and cost containment.

Rand Research Review
P.O. Box 2138
Santa Monica, CA 90406-2138
(213) 393-0411
Three times a year. Free.

The Rand Corporation is a private, nonprofit institution engaged in research and analysis of matters affecting national security and public welfare, including health-related research. Some issues of the newsletter may not be related to health care.

State Health Notes
Intergovernmental Health Policy Project
2011 I Street, NW, Suite 200
Washington, DC 20006
(202) 872-1445
Ten issues a year. $95.

This newsletter published by the Intergovernmental Health Policy Project at George Washington University provides information about health policy and program activities of the 50 states. Each issue includes a column based on interviews with leading health policymakers.

State Legislatures
National Conference of State Legislatures
Marketing Department
1560 Broadway, Suite 700
Denver, CO 80202
(303) 830-2200
Ten times a year. $49 a year; single copy $5.25.

This journal of the National Conference of State Legislatures provides comprehensive information on state-level government and policy. Health care is not covered in every issue, but is a frequent topic. Many aspects of the health care crisis are being addressed on a state-by-state basis, which makes this journal a valuable resource.

Wellness Management
National Wellness Association
South Hall, 1319 Fremont Street
Stevens Point, WI 54481-3899
(715) 346-2172
Quarterly. Free to members.

This newsletter is published by the National Wellness Association to inform its members about recent developments, resources, programming, events, and educational opportunities in the wellness and health promotion fields.

7

Nonprint Resources

THIS CHAPTER LISTS NONPRINT SOURCES of information on the health care crisis, including computer databases and videotapes.

Online Databases

MEDLARS®

Type: Reference (bibliographic)
Producer: National Library of Medicine
              Building 38, Room 4N421
              8600 Rockville Pike
              Bethesda, MD 20894
              (800) 638-8480

Many of the MEDLARS databases are designed for the use of health care professionals researching specific health problems. The best known is MEDLINE®, which enables computer queries to the National Library of Medicine's computer store of journal article references on specific topics. Besides MEDLINE, which became operational in 1971 and currently contains six million references going back to 1966, the system offers 25 other databases. The general researcher might be interested in some of the less technical, more broadly based databases, such as BIOETHICSLINE®, which offers bibliographic citations covering ethics and related public policy issues in health care and biomedical research. Also of general interest are HEALTH®, which covers health planning and administration, and HISTLINE®, which covers the history of medicine and related sciences.

Videotapes

The following are documentary and informational videos on topics related to the health care crisis, as well as sources for further information. Many of the organizations listed in Chapter 5 offer videos in their publications catalogs. The National Library of Medicine publishes an annual audiovisuals catalog that has numerous listings in the health care category.

The Coming of Age in America
Type: VHS
Length: 30 min.
Date: 1988
Cost: $24.95
Source: National Council on the Aging, Inc.
            Dept. 5087
            600 Maryland Avenue, SW
            West Wing 100
            Washington, DC 20061-5087

Narrated by Willard Scott, this videotape answers questions and provides fresh information on developments in the long-term-care field. It points out that the U.S. population is aging rapidly, leading to a host of health care problems, including the need for adequate long-term care. It includes interviews with public policy experts, legislators, health care providers, and private financial planners.

Does Doctor Know Best?
Type: 3/4″, 1/2″
Length: 60 min.
Date: 1989
Cost: $29.95
Source: Annenberg/CPB Project
            901 E Street, NW
            Washington, DC 20004
            (202) 879-9600

A part of the Columbia University seminars on media and society titled Ethics in America, this thought-provoking videotape features a panel of medical experts discussing the ethics of doctor-patient relationships. Using the case of a young woman who is diagnosed as having cancer and who subsequently becomes pregnant, the panelists discuss how much the patient should be told, who is in charge of choosing medical treatment, and whether doctors should allow their patients to commit suicide.

The Human Experiment

Type:	3/4″, 1/2″
Length:	60 min.
Date:	1988
Cost:	$29.95
Source:	Annenberg/CPB Project
	901 E Street, NW
	Washington, DC 20004
	(202) 879-9600

A part of the Columbia University seminars on media and society titled Ethics in America, this excellent videotape features a panel of medical experts and a U.S. Supreme Court justice discussing the ethics of medical research. The panelists consider how competition for prizes and profits may lead to secrecy and lack of cooperation. They also debate the need to test new drugs balanced against the needs of people desperate for treatment.

The Human Experiment

Type:	3/4″, 1/2″
Length:	60 min.
Date:	1989
Cost:	$29.95
Source:	Annenberg/CPB Project
	901 E Street, NW
	Washington, DC 20004
	(202) 879-9600

A part of the Columbia University seminars on media and society titled Ethics in America, this videotape features a panel of ethical and medical experts discussing whether it is ethical to risk the life of one patient today to save the lives of many others in the future. A hypothetical case of a man with AIDS is presented.

Malpractice

Type:	VHS
Length:	60 min.
Date:	1985
Cost:	$85
Source:	Columbia University Seminars on
	Media and Society
	475 Riverside Drive, Suite 248
	New York, NY 10115
	(212) 280-3666

A part of the Columbia University seminars on media and society titled Managing Our Miracles, this videotape features a panel of lawyers, doctors, and ethicists discussing the crisis in malpractice insurance. It follows the hypothetical case of a child damaged at birth through a large court award given for malpractice. Although a variety of opinions are represented, the current legal system is highly criticized by a number of panelists.

Prescriptions for Profit

Type: VHS
Length: 60 min.
Date: 1989
Cost: $300
Source: PBS
             1320 Braddock Place
             Alexandria, VA 22314-1698
             (800) 424-7963

This *Frontline* program is a scathing exposé of the prescription industry, whose profits equal $30 billion a year. Concentrating on pain relievers, this videotape investigates various arthritis medications, showing how far some drug companies go to make a profit. *Prescriptions for Profit* is suitable for both consumers and health care professionals.

The Right To Die . . . The Choice Is Yours

Type: VHS
Length: 14 min.
Date: 1987
Cost: $38
Source: Society for the Right to Die
             250 West 57th Street
             New York, NY 10107
             (212) 246-6962

This videotape explains the individual's right to refuse treatment by filling out a living will in advance of a medical emergency. Details are given on how to fill out a living will, including specific life-prolonging procedures an individual might include in such a document.

Setting Limits

Type: 3/4", 1/2"
Length: 47 min.
Date: 1988
Cost: $200
Source: Medical University of South Carolina
             Division of Continuing Education
             171 Ashley Avenue
             Charleston, SC 29425
             (803) 792-4435

This thought-provoking lecture by Daniel Callahan deals with the question of an aging population in a society with finite economic abilities to provide expensive health care. It asks numerous questions, such as what the goals of old age will be in the future and what entails a "full" life. Also addressed is whether medicine should continue to advance in acute care or whether chronic care will be more important.

What Legislators Need To Know about Medical Malpractice

Type: VHS
Length: 26 min.
Date: 1985
Cost: $35
Source: National Conference of State Legislatures
             1560 Broadway, Suite 700
             Denver, CO 80202
             (303) 830-2200

This videotape defines malpractice and airs criticism of the current system from the point of view of lawyers, legislators, insurers, doctors, and academicians. Recommendations are made on how state legislatures might try to solve this problem. Although designed for legislators, this videotape is useful for anyone seeking information about the many sides of this controversial, complex issue.

What Price Miracles?

Type: 3/4" U-matic
Length: 29 min.
Date: 1980
Cost: $205
Source: Pennsylvania State University
             Audiovisual Services
             University Park, PA 16802
             (814) 865-6314

Who Lives, Who Dies, Who Decides

Type: VHS
Length: 156 min.
Date: 1986
Cost: $160
Source: California Pacific Medical Center
             Division of Education
             P.O. Box 7999
             San Francisco, CA 94120
             (415) 923-3440

Ted Koppel facilitates a panel of experts handling phone calls on controversial questions in medical ethics. The panelists discuss whether rationing medical care is a viable way of controlling costs. The panel also considers how we can keep a humane tradition when human choices are governed by technology and whether technology is the cause or the cure of rising costs.

Other Guides to Nonprint Resources

In the sources listed below, many of the listings under "health care" and "medicine" are disease specific or deal with such topics as first aid, personal hygiene, or nutrition. However, all of the sources do include some general topics related to a broader view of health care such as cost containment or ethics.

Journal Graphics: The Television Transcript Company Topics Catalog. Journal Graphics, Inc., 267 Broadway, New York, NY 10007.

Journal Graphics produces written transcripts of over 30 nationally broadcast television shows and specials. Health and medicine are among the topics covered. Fees for most transcripts range from $3 to $4.

National Library of Medicine Audiovisuals Catalog. National Library of Medicine, 8600 Rockville Pike, Bethesda, MD 20894. Annual cumulation (1977–). ISSN 0149-9939.

Published quarterly, with the fourth issue being the annual cumulation, this comprehensive reference lists audiovisual materials and microcomputer software available through the National Library of Medicine. Entries are categorized by title and subject for both monographs and serials. Selected titles are available on interlibrary loan to libraries in the United States.

Sources: A Guide to Print and Nonprint Materials Available from Organizations, Industry, Government Agencies, and Specialized Publishers. Gaylord Professional Publications, P.O. Box 61, Syracuse, NY 13201. Three times a year. $60 a year.

Published in association with Neal-Schuman Publishers, this publication includes "Index to Free and Inexpensive Materials."

Video Rating Guide for Libraries. Santa Barbara, CA: ABC-CLIO, Inc., 1990–. $89.50 a year.

This quarterly guide reviews and rates VHS-format videos, including topics on medicine and health. There are subject, title, and audience indexes in each issue, cumulated annually in the October issue.

The Video Source Book. Detroit: Gale Research Inc., 1989. $199.

Compiled from distributor and producer information, this reference covers videos in all formats. Entries are presented in alphabetical order by title and include brief annotations. It is indexed by subject and main category.

Glossary

AHA American Hospital Association. The major professional organization representing hospitals and hospital-related health care facilities and organizations. (See Chapter 5.)

AMA American Medical Association. The major professional organization representing physicians. (See Chapter 5.)

bioethics The moral aspects of modern health care, ranging from the right to live to the right to die. Bioethics cover conflicts between medicine and religion, between medicine and money, and so on.

capitation A method of reimbursement in which a provider of health care receives a fixed fee per person from a defined population for a period of time, regardless of the number of services used by the enrollee. HMOs are the predominant form of this arrangement.

CAT, CT Computerized tomography. A diagnostic machine that can distinguish one soft tissue from another. The scanner uses several x-ray tubes simultaneously from different angles. Each tube sees its own small pattern of densities, which the computer puts into a cross section.

DRGs Diagnosis-related groups. A set of categories based on patient diagnosis, procedures, and age. These categories are assigned for the purposes of hospital reimbursement under Medicare.

euthanasia The medical term used to describe the deliberate ending of the life of an individual for merciful reasons.

fee for service This is the reimbursement pattern of traditional medicine, where the provider charges a fee for each separate service and the payment is made after the service is provided.

for-profit health care Health care provided by a corporation whose surplus income is paid to those who own or have invested in the corporation.

HCFA The U.S. Health Care Financing Administration is the agency responsible for Medicare and federal involvement in Medicaid. It is a part of the U.S. Department of Health and Human Services.

health insurance Insurance that offers protection to consumers against medical expenses. This protection is given in return for a fixed, predetermined premium. It usually covers hospital and professional fees, but not preventive care.

HMOs Health maintenance organizations are prepaid providers of health care. The organization assumes the financial risk for the care provided to enrolled members. Members will be reimbursed only if they receive care from the HMO. A key feature is the combination of the functions of insurance and delivery within one organization. The HMO assumes the contractual responsibility for providing a stated range of health care services. The definition of HMOs has expanded to include individual practice associations (IPAs), preferred provider organizations (PPOs), and group and network organizations that contract with physician group practices to provide HMO-style care to members at one or more locations.

Medicaid A health insurance program jointly shared by the federal government and the states. It provides care for poor Americans and is administered mainly by state governments. Because states have considerable discretion in defining eligibility standards, eligibility for Medicaid varies widely from state to state.

Medicare A national insurance program for Americans who are over age 65 or disabled. The HCFA administers this program, which covers hospital expenses, physicians, and other professional services.

national health insurance A program in which government provides health insurance for all citizens. Various forms of national health insurance exist in virtually all developed countries, but not in the United States.

NIH National Institutes of Health. One of the world's foremost biomedical research centers, NIH is located in Bethesda, Maryland. (See Chapter 5.)

PPOs Preferred provider organizations are usually designated by a company to provide employee insurance. The providers receive payment on a discounted, fee-for-service basis. Employees are given incentives (such as no coinsurance) to use the providers within the PPO, but may seek covered services from outside the system.

PROs Professional review organizations are private, for-profit companies staffed by physicians, nurses, and other health care professionals. They contract with the federal government to review hospital cases to monitor the cost and quality of care received by Medicare beneficiaries.

self-insurance In this arrangement, an employer acts as a health insurer by paying employees' medical expenses directly rather than paying their insurance premiums. The administration of such plans is contracted out by most employers.

Index